HOLDING TIME

the practice of

INK & ASANA

SOMATIC WRITING, YOGA, AND THE ART OF
CREATING SPACE

LAURA C. COLE

WRITE. FLOW. TRANSFORM.

I&A | Write. Flow. Transform.

Holding Time: the Practice of Ink & Asana

Hardcover ISBN: 978-1-960491-17-6

Paperback ISBN: 978-1-960491-27-5

eBook ISBN: 978-1-960491-32-9

ALSO BY LAURA COLE

The Yoga Sequencing Journal
The Be Mindful Journal
The Be Happy Journal
The Be Well Journal
The Be Well Journal Volume 2
The Dream Big Journal

To Ricky,

for absolutely everything.

CONTENTS

INTRODUCTION

We are all living archives, carrying the weight of a thousand untold stories in our bodies and in our bones. They are our legacy. If we haven't yet found the words to release them, they may feel like they are slipping away—memories of those we love, days to be celebrated, life-pivoting moments. But they are there, and our bodies hold the key to freeing them. With the right tools, we can carefully sift through the stories, isolate them, and bring them into the light, excavating like archaeologists digging into the past.

My mother was a passionate and lifelong genealogist. She would spend hours and days in various archives, doing her own kind of digging, looking for that one piece of a story that would explain so much. She understood that we know who we are when we know where we came from. But not every story is told in an archive, and we can find so much of what we're looking for inside ourselves. That gift lives within us.

There is a sanctuary that exists between a mindful inhale and a slow exhale. It is the middle of a lifelong breath. Some relationships are like that: eternal—a connection so deep it has always been, and always will be. Your time, and your story, are simply what I call the Middle of Always. By opening the creaky attic trunk of our history and celebrating that bond, we honor that sacred story. Whether writing together as a pair, or remembering a loved one who has left us, we anchor the most vital elements of legacy.

My own excavation began in a moment of forced stillness—and in that stillness, I realized that to face my future, I first had to walk back into my past. I had made the desperate, difficult decision to intentionally become sick. After years of research, frustration, wild goose chases, and doctors who dismissed my symptoms, I had zeroed in on what I thought caused my mysterious and once-debilitating illness. The thing was, to confirm my suspicion, I was going to have to make the condition show up on a blood test. That meant eating foods that would cause my symptoms to spiral out of control, and that road carried a ton of PTSD for me.

Over the years, through ups and downs, experimentation, and elimination testing, I'd made several discoveries that had helped me, like yoga and removing certain foods from my diet. These were not your run-of-the-mill food sensitivities; no, these foods triggered something awful in me, which I believed to be an autoimmune disease. To be sure, my dietary changes had helped quite a bit, but I still wanted answers. Actually, I needed them. I was no longer okay with not knowing exactly what it was, and I had information that I believed would finally give me an answer—would get me to the truth. I had to start a "gluten challenge"—a term used for those who go back on a gluten diet in order for antibodies to show up on a blood test that detects celiac disease.

I realized I had to go back into the fire to find the truth. I knew I had to face this moment with a bit of grit and a bit of grace. Instead of running away from my illness, I knew I must finally take a closer look at everything I was carrying, and that included the deepest grief.

Seven years before I decided to embark on this wild ride, I had lost my mother to cancer. She had been my confidant, the primary keeper of my history, and the woman who had helped me navigate every previous ailment. She was my guide, and my source of reason and pure love. I wasn't just missing her care; I was missing her wisdom. I had to go into a dark cave alone, with no one to hold the light.

I needed her more than ever during this time. I was scared and overwhelmed. But she was gone, and I had to go on this arduous journey without her. I missed her terribly, and my grief was more pronounced now that I'd decided to dive face-first back into the trauma I'd long feared would return one day. I didn't know how I was going to do this without her.

I was making myself ready. I leaned into my lifeline: my yoga practice. In the twelve years since the worst of my symptoms had settled into an acceptable new normal, I knew exactly how yoga could help me. But when I'd first come to yoga, I was lost, and here I was—lost again. My stress levels were up, my breathing short, my appetite down. This was familiar, and I knew it was time to step on the mat.

My daily practice had subsided a bit by this time. I was now practicing yoga two to three days out of the week, including teaching online. Respectable, sure, since there's no "what good looks like" when it comes to a meaningful practice. But knowing what I know about myself, my health, and my need for that release that settles into my bones in Savasana, getting back to a daily practice was what I needed.

It was raining outside, the water gently pattering against the window of my yoga room. The sky looked like I felt, casting a gray mood over my sanctuary. I kept a small collection of mats in the closet, and I took out the yellow one, a color that always reminds me of Mom. I slowly rolled up the green mat that had been lying on the floor and placed it in the closet in the empty space I'd just made. The yellow Jade mat was newer, fresh and bright. I carefully laid it down on the floor, lining it up so that the top of the mat was facing the window.

Here. Now.

I stepped to the front of the mat. I drank in a deep breath, and let it out through an open mouth. I looked down, aligning my big toes. My hands floated down by my sides on the out breath. I started to inhale slowly as my hands swept out to the sides and up, stretching toward the sky. I rooted down strongly through my feet, getting taller and taller as I reached. When I'd brought in all of the breath that I could, I gradually exhaled as my palms came together. I drew my hands down, slowly, slowly, until they were resting in front of my heart. I closed my eyes. rising up onto the balls of my feet, centering myself, and rested my heels back down.

I began.

Sun salutations, I am warm.
Standing pose flows, I am graceful.
Strengthening sequence, I am powerful.
Backbending stretches, I am open.
Forward folds, I am humble.
Twisting side to side, I am balanced.
I drink in each breath. I am here. Now.
The world has fallen away.

At the end of my practice, I lay in Savasana. Tension: gone. All hard work: over. My head was clear as I sank deeper and deeper into the Earth, allowing the ground to hold me. I had nowhere to go and nothing to do but exist in the middle of that lifelong breath. Relaxing… sinking… In the silence of that sanctuary came my truth: the missing. And then: the path.

Write to her.

It was just the softest whisper of a thought, yet it landed with the weight of a stone. I almost gasped. I didn't just hear it; I felt it in my bones. If my body held the clues from my past and the keys to my future, then she and I would explore the stories in ink. I instantly knew it was the answer I needed. A small smile curled my lip, as a tear left my eye, rolled past my ear, and fell onto the mat. I lay there breathing deep into my belly for another minute or two. Easing out of Savasana by drawing my knees into my chest, I gave them a little squeeze. I rocked up to a seated position, and placed the top of my right foot on top of my left thigh, up by my hip, crossing my legs into half lotus position. I rested the backs of my hands on my knees, palms open to the sky—ready to receive. My eyes were closed as I took a deep breath and slowly let it out. I knew now that I would write letters to my mother during the months I had to undergo this challenge. That is exactly what I needed. She would come with me on this journey, because of course she would.

And so that's what I did. I started writing letters to my late mother while I was in agony over having to walk back into the trauma, the pain, the insomnia. And as I did so, something slowly started to shift. My keyboard became my time machine, my therapist, my vehicle. As my body endured the slow but sure return of the worst of my symptoms, I started writing down memories of our time together. I did it to feel closer to Mom, to finally tell our stories, just as she had asked me to—but before I knew it, I was writing chapters. The process did more than just tell my story; it curated my history.

My somatic movement practice (yoga) was the grounding force that propelled me forward. It was in quiet moments on the mat, after having connected my mind and body, that I could see my memories clearly. I wasn't just doing yoga anymore. I wasn't just writing. I was learning how to hold time. I realized that by threading the memory of my mother through my own fingers at the keyboard, I was anchoring her legacy into the present. I wasn't just writing a memoir; I was building a fortress of our time together that death couldn't touch. All of the memories that had faded, and the ones that I'd long feared would be lost, came into vivid focus.

A book fell out of me over the course of two months. It was as if I was taking my grief and trauma into the light, rinsing them in the clarity I'd been given, until only the most sacred artifacts of our legacy remained. My connection to my mother was stronger than ever, and it fueled me with the power I needed to get through to the answers I longed for about my health. That book is my memoir and a labor of pure love. It was a major work of discovery, and as I write this, I am contemplating whether to publish it, a deeply personal and difficult choice.

The book you hold in your hands is not about how to get published—there are lots of those books out there. This book is about experiencing the amazing transformation that comes from writing your story—the pure, unbridled joy that comes from integrating your history or from celebrating an eternal bond and letting that relationship live forever, in ink. It's also about using the power of yoga to inspire you to write that story.

It doesn't matter how you do it, and it doesn't matter what you do with it when you're done. Your story could be journal entries for you alone, and that's beautiful and perfect if that is your choice. It could be something you share with family only, as part of your legacy. Or you could choose to share it with the world. You don't have to worry about that now, and when it comes time to decide, whatever you do, don't let what others might think take away any of the joy and pure expansiveness you found in the process.

The transformative power of moving a story from the sanctuary of the body to the clarity of the page astounded me. As I continued to deepen my yoga practice, going within helped me get clarity at the keyboard. At the same time, my yoga practice erased the noise from my head and allowed me to find focus to write, giving me the peace and space I needed to create. I found that writing not only released the stories from my mind and body; it moved them through my heart, honoring them. It completely transformed how I viewed my past, grief, loss, and illness. I then took a renewed sense of grace and forgiveness back to the mat. My yoga practice became deeper than ever.

These two ancient practices were intersecting, weaving together, and creating a beautiful work of art—of growth and self-discovery—that left me illuminated and wanting more. Over time, the two practices have become one, and part of my daily life.

Our journey together throughout this book is not about being the most advanced yogi out there, or the best writer. The transformation we seek is achieved through just doing the work. By showing up and engaging in practice, you'll find the best *you*, setting free the stories your body holds, so that you can make new ones.

So, that's what we're here to do together. We'll explore both writing and yoga in ways unexpected and unique to each individual yogi/writer. This is not a yoga manual that will teach you how to do each pose, although I will share a sampling of techniques I recommend you use to get the most out of them. We'll be talking about how to practice yoga in a way that fuels creativity, helps you create clarity and peace, and write your story so that it too can be excavated, preserving and honoring your history. Your yoga and your writing will inform each other, intertwining in a powerful and healing way. Your writing may be completely unlike what I described above. Perhaps you're starting or continuing a meaningful journaling practice and have no intention of writing a book. Maybe you have expertise or a message to send out in a non-fiction book of your own. Or you could have a story to tell the world, your memoir itching to get out of you, but it needs space to grow and bloom. Whatever writing goals you have or writing style you're interested in, it doesn't matter—the art of it, the expression, the venting is what will heal you and set you on the road to transformation.

You don't have to try to transform. It will just happen through practice. One day, you'll look back and marvel at what has happened.

Such a combined practice sets the practitioner on a new path, one of purpose and openness. Watch how writing and yoga can profoundly influence each other's creative and expansive power. In doing so, you'll find your way to creating positive change—not only in your own life, but in the world. What you'll get out of the pages that follow is a holistic approach to personal growth, creativity, and self-discovery, the benefits of which to the mind, body, and spirit are only limited by your commitment to the work. I'll also share my journey as an accidental memoirist—how opening the vault in search of one story unexpectedly unlocked a wellspring of others. I found the creative process so fulfilling that ideas for more books just keep coming. Once you unlock the writer in you, they just keep showing up. An integrated writing and yoga practice is an outlet for all I have to say, but more than that, it creates an inner world of fulfillment, forgiveness, and grace that I never knew I could have access to. It was also a way to process the trauma I held about my run-in with a mysterious illness, and my grief over the loss of my grandmother and mother, so much so that it changed how I saw all of that—in a way that each singular practice couldn't have accomplished. The merging of the two changed me forever, and I sincerely hope that you will find that as well.

There is no wrong way to begin. Step on the mat. Sit in front of your open journal or keyboard. Select the ideas, bits, and pieces you'll take away from this book, and make them your own. Your way is the right way.

When you purposefully become the caretaker of your own history, you naturally begin to send that strength and wisdom out to those you love and the world beyond. The peace you find at the center of your practice has a ripple effect—quiet changes that begin with you.

For if you and I can anchor even just one memory of our most cherished and eternal loves, then we have honored what the Middle of Always. I know this to be true because of the power of the moment I first held the weight of my own completed manuscript. As I looked down at the pages—the stories of my mom and me—I realized that the ink had done what the mind alone could not. I was no longer chasing just a memory; I was holding our time in my hands.

HOW TO USE THIS BOOK

Welcome to *Holding Time*, your somatic guide to honoring your most sacred bonds and your own history. Here, we weave the practices of somatic writing (ink) and the wisdom of yoga (asana) into a holistic and singular path to discovery. This book is designed as an interactive journey, inviting you not just to read but to actively engage with the material and apply its principles to your daily life.

THE SOMATIC BRIDGE: FROM MOVEMENT TO MEMORY

You will see the word somatic throughout these pages. It comes from the Greek word soma, which means the living body. In this practice, somatic is more than a term; it is our gateway.

To work somatically is to acknowledge that your stories don't live in your head. They live in your nervous system, your breath, and in your bones. When we practice Ink & Asana, we aren't just thinking about the past. We're listening to the body's collection of hard-won lessons and taking its dictation. We are moving the body to find the story and expressing it in ink, giving it a home.

In this practice, we don't do yoga to get "better" at a pose; we do yoga to become a better listener to our own bodies and our own histories.

The body is a master at storing our "stuff." It tucks stories into the tight spaces of our hips, the tension in our shoulders, and the restricted depth of our breath. Through asana (poses), we gently create space to expand out of our stress-wrapped physicality. As the muscles lengthen and the joints open, the stories are unlocked and invited to move. You aren't just stretching, you're clearing the path for memories and ideas.

Between the movement and the writing is the echo phase of the pose, when the body and mind are open. This is where a somatic sensation (heart beating, palms relaxing) begins to move into thought. By finding stillness, we allow the whispers of the body to become clear enough to hear. That's why I heard *write to her* as I lay in Savasana.

Once the story has reached the surface, we can take it to our writing. Because the body is now open and the nervous system is more calm, writing becomes less of a struggle. The breath expands out through the hand and the ink becomes an extension of it. You are simply pouring out what the yoga has loosened. As it arrives on the screen or paper, it is anchored there, and held fast for later examination. It may be a precious memory, an innovative idea, or the deepest gratitude. Slowing down inside allows us the space to explore, expand, and find the joy that lives inside of us, always. We just have to dive in to go get it.

MAKING THE MOST OF YOUR PRACTICE

Embrace the "Put It into Practice" Sections:

Throughout *Holding Time*, you'll find dedicated "Put It into Practice" sections. These are exercises that will help you deepen your yoga practice and create a nourishing writing journey. Take your time working through them, selecting the items you wish to complete, and maybe coming back later to work on them. Each section is specifically designed to help you integrate the philosophical concepts and techniques discussed in the preceding chapter into your practice. Think of them as your personal laboratory for experimentation and application.

By actively engaging with these exercises, you'll deepen your understanding, develop new habits, and truly embody the teachings of *Holding Time.*

Do the work, and you'll unlock the many benefits outlined in these pages.

BONUS Materials and Free Video Library:

Come join our community! To further enhance your understanding and provide a direct experience of the yoga practices, writing prompts, and meditations discussed, a free video library has been created to support concepts mentioned throughout the book. These videos allow us to spend a little time together and offer visual guidance, allowing you to flow through jmovements and meditations that support the material in this book with instruction.

To practice with me, gain instant access to all the videos, and begin your embodied learning, please visit **www.inkandasana.com/ book-bonus** This video library is your toolkit, allowing you to seamlessly move from reading about the practices to actively performing them. You'll also find links to two optional journals: *The Ink & Asana Journal* and *The S.E.E.D.S Journal.* The first is a blank journal to use alongside this book. The second is what you'll use after you finish *Holding Time* to help you integrate your Ink & Asana practice into daily life.

Engage with the Material Actively:

Holding Time is not meant for passive consumption. Consider it a companion and a guide. Also, I recommend that you keep a dedicated journal or notebook with you as you read.

Feel free to use any blank journal or notebook as your dedicated writing space for the prompts in this book. Use it to complete the "Put It into Practice" exercises, record your reflections, explore insights that arise during your yoga and writing sessions, and track your progress.

☐ Throughout this book, you'll find these little checkboxes next to activities you can complete and actions you can take. I recommend circling them when you see something you want to try, then coming back and checking it off once you complete it. It's oh so satisfying!

There are a lot of writing prompts throughout this book that will help you deepen your yoga and writing practice, but don't feel like you have to do them all at once. Take your time, select the ones you'd like to try, then come back to them when you're ready.

The principles and practices outlined here are simply offerings. Experiment with different techniques, adapt them to fit your unique needs and lifestyle, and discover what resonates most deeply with you. There's no "wrong" way to practice; your way is the right way. That's true in yoga, writing, and the use of this book.

Enjoy the Ride:

Holding Time will take you on a journey of the self, inviting you to explore the intersection of ancient wisdom and your own brand of creativity. Be patient with yourself, mindfully celebrate small victories, and remember that both yoga and writing are *practices*—always evolving and offering new ways to explore the deep ocean that is your inner world.

It is a privilege to guide you through this journey of excavation. We are here to honor the truth of our histories and, in doing so, create a ripple of grace that reaches far beyond our own lives. Through one mindful pose and one honest word at a time, we begin the sacred work of preserving the middle of always.

DISCLAIMER

xxiii

The advice and insights shared in this book, particularly in the chapters discussing difficult memories, grief, and trauma, are drawn from the author's personal experience and understanding of writing as a tool for self-discovery and emotional processing. The author is not a trained psychologist, therapist, or mental health professional. This book is not intended to provide psychological or medical advice, diagnosis, or treatment. If you are struggling with illness, trauma, grief, or mental health challenges, please consult with a qualified professional. The practices described herein are meant to support creative expression and personal reflection, and should not replace professional guidance.

PART I

FOUNDATIONS

Mind and Body, Pen and Page

THE PATH OF THE BODY
Yoga as the Foundation

We'll start with yoga, just because that's where I started. You might be someone who does yoga every day, and you're here to find inspiring ways to deepen your practice, and add a writing component. Perhaps you're a current or aspiring yoga teacher, here to add to your toolkit. Or maybe you're a casual yogi, looking to expand your understanding. Wherever you are in your journey, there's ample ancient wisdom to apply to your current practice, and make it even deeper.

It's my absolute joy that you're here, however you've arrived. Come to yoga any way you want to. If you're here for exercise, great. If you feel a need to slow your nervous system and learn skills that will help you relax, you're also in the right place. Perhaps you were perfectly healthy when you arrived in this community, or maybe, like me, not so much. The amazing thing about yoga and this collective of beautiful souls is that it's for all of us, and there's a deep and meaningful—and healing—practice for everyone and every body. We all come to yoga in our own way, but if we make a study of not only the asanas, but also the philosophies and principles the ancient yogis established, we end up making a study of ourselves.

You know as well as I do, that the mind and body are inextricably connected: when you relax one, the other follows. Then one builds on the other. And all that physical work that goes into the poses? It's through that exertion that our tissues start to release, and then the mind marches in step right behind. When that happens, that's when the real yoga begins. That's the magic that keeps us coming back for more.

At its core, yoga isn't a workout. It's a journey of the physical on the way to the emotional, the mind–body, and the spiritual. It's a path. It's a philosophy and a science, designed to bring peace and fitness to your body, mind, and spirit.

In this chapter, we'll journey beyond the mat to explore some yoga basics: the philosophy and true yoga. This may be a review for you—a reinforcement to help you refocus your intentions and deepen your practice. We'll explore the power of the breath, the practice of mindfulness, and how these core principles can transform how you go out into the world and deal with the crazy messiness that is life. But we're here in the context of blending our yoga practice with writing, so as you go through this chapter, take a fresh eye to the basic foundations of yogic philosophy and think how you'll apply them not only to a refreshed practice on the mat, but to a new practice on the page. Take a seat on your mat, or in a chair, and get comfy. We're about to dive into the ancient wisdom that's more relevant today than ever.

BEYOND THE PHYSICAL: ASANA IS THE WAY IN

When I first came to yoga, I was in a pure trauma state. When I look back, I think of it almost as animalistic—pure physical taking over everything. I had a need, and I wasn't even sure yoga would fulfill it. I just needed *something* to help. My body had mysteriously started to fail, and I was in a great deal of pain. I could hardly sleep, I couldn't eat much, and I'd lost too much weight. I visited many doctors, none of whom could figure out what was wrong with me, and all of whom actually gave up on me: they threw up their hands, sending me away with a guess and a prescription. It was insulting, the implication being that it was in my head. Admittedly, them writing me off as likely hysterical, got in a little, and I thought maybe I really was just losing my mind. Deep down though, I knew it was my body, and that there must be a way to ease both. I wanted a holistic solution, so I kept searching.

Going in and through the body, we cool the mind; it's why yoga is such a lifeline for some, and a way of life for so many. The ancient yogis tapped into one of the most valuable resources ever discovered: the ability of the body to heal the mind. The link between the two, when tended to like a garden, plants little self-care seeds, and lets embodied peace, creativity, wisdom, and joy grow.

I knew precisely none of that back then. I just thought I should put my body in a relaxed state as much as possible. I'd done very little yoga at that point, and I didn't really know much about it. But even though I was so very weak and tired, I thought I would give it a try to see if it would at least calm my nervous system enough to help me sleep.

I went online and found a yoga platform with many teachers. Almost immediately, I lucked out and found a Yin Yoga teacher, Bernie Clark. I landed on Yin Yoga because it's the slowest of the slow yoga. I had literally Googled, "what is the slowest, most relaxing yoga." Yin, as Bernie says, is the "other half" of your yoga practice. You've heard of yin/yang, right? Yin and yang represent the concept of duality in ancient Chinese philosophy, signifying two opposite but interconnected forces that exist in harmony and complement each other. Yin is soft, allowing, still, passive, slow, cooling, yielding, and introspective. Conversely, yang is associated with words like active, bright, warm, light, and the sun. Sometimes, other types of yoga, like Vinyasa, are referred to as more yang yoga.

Yin Yoga is not to be confused with Restorative Yoga, which is also relaxing and slow, often taught with candlelight and soft music, and deeply sedative. I also sought out classes like these, but Bernie's scientific approach to Yin Yoga and the deep opening of the body's tissues resonated with me at the time.

Yin Yoga was exactly what I needed, and I started practicing every day, sometimes twice a day. I decided to set up our spare room as a place to do yoga as I settled into a daily practice. I painted the walls a light green color and kept the decor minimal, trying to calm my nervous system in every way possible. The classes were long and slow, as we held each pose for three to five minutes each. And they were all done on the floor—there are no standing poses in Yin Yoga. The long hold is to help us get into the connective tissues. Whereas more yang forms of yoga work the muscles, Yin Yoga works on your connective tissues, so you need long, static poses to work into them. And during those long poses, Bernie would talk. To keep our minds from wandering too far, he would tell us the science behind the poses, and how we were breathing deeply not just to open the body but to activate the parasympathetic nervous system.

It started to work. I felt myself begin to feel some relief, if not yet heal. At the very least, I knew I wasn't alone and that some of what I was going through was certainly common. And when I later discovered dietary habits that allowed my symptoms to begin to retreat, my yoga practice became ever deeper. As the physical pain and fatigue started to subside, I found myself wanting to know more about why yoga was so helpful, and how I could go even further, beyond the physical, and begin to heal my heart and worried mind. For I still didn't know what was "wrong" with me. I was seeking wisdom and hope.

I started reading, and a whole world opened up to me.

We're all familiar with the physical form of yoga: the poses (asanas), and the stretching and strength-building aspects of the practice. But the term **yoga** has been widely translated as "union with the divine," the meaning of which is unique to the individual student: divine, as in the divine self, or God, or the highest power you know, whatever that means to you. One of the most beautiful aspects of yoga is that it doesn't tell you what to believe in a spiritual sense; instead, it provides the tools for you to explore your spirituality in your own way.

The term **union** is also used to mean the union of body and mind. Chin mudra, a hand gesture you often see when a yogi is sitting in meditation where the tip of the thumb and forefinger touch with the rest of the fingers outstretched or relaxed, is representative of this union. It's a reminder that as the digits touch, body and mind connect. It's a way to "drop in" and find your center, even subconsciously reminding yourself of that connection.

Why is the mind–body connection so important? Nothing brings us into the present moment like connecting with the body. It IS the here and now. When we're attuned to our physical being, we bring the mind into focus on what is real, and right now. We tend to live all up in our skulls, worrying about the future, reliving the past; so when we jump into the present, we leave all of that behind and focus on what's important in the moment. And not only that: we will all deal with a physical ailment, illness, or injury at some point in our lives. Learning to be in tune with the body makes you an attentive passenger inside your physiology, which will make you more likely to find relief and healing.

Yoga has also been given the profound, and I think apt, meaning of "remembering," suggesting a return to our true, inherent nature. It's a homecoming, connecting us back to our innate wholeness, embodied peace, and something larger than ourselves. So when we practice yoga, we aren't acquiring something new but instead going within to remove the conditioning of society, the distractions of the external, and the influence of the ego. When we do so, we find what has been there all along. This remembering happens through consistent practice; moments of clarity and stillness provide a way of reconnecting with our deepest self, of recognizing our authentic being.

When I first heard that yoga can be defined as "remembering," it felt so real, so right. For me, yoga created a feeling of coming home to something I'd always needed. Not just the asanas, but the space they created within. Not to mention, there's so much welcoming from the yoga community at large as well as the founding yogis—an invitation to learn the wisdom of the ancient. This is so important in our newer cultures in the West, where wisdom is so very absent. Older cultures have found so much of what humans naturally seek and created foundational concepts that can be adapted and built upon. Spreading that eternal wisdom from culture to culture, especially with a focus on pure enlightenment and positive change in the world, surely can be nothing other than good—especially if we're true to yoga's origins and respect, always honoring, its teachings and masters.

The history of yoga is a rich one, full of handed-down wisdom and beauty from teacher to student. Yoga's long lineage and wide international reach make it continue to evolve and grow. Teachers make additions, get creative in their sequencing, and bring their own flavor to the practices they teach, intertwining their unique blend of inspiration, themes, and cues into the genealogy of yoga. And some of those teachers pass their methods and knowledge on to new teachers, who eventually do the same. The traditional philosophy is vast and serves as a toolkit for navigating the wild ride that is life.

Yoga is an ancient practice that originated in northern India thousands of years ago. It didn't come into being from a single event or person, but rather evolved over time through various spiritual traditions and practices. The first written mention of the word "yoga" appeared in the *Vedas*, the oldest sacred texts of Hinduism. Over centuries, these ideas were refined and developed by sages, who documented their beliefs in texts like the *Upanishads* and the *Bhagavad Gita*. It was during the Classical Period (between about 200 B.C. to 500 A.D.) that the sage Patanjali compiled and systematized these ancient teachings into the *Yoga Sutras*, which described the "Eight Limbs of Yoga" and are considered the foundation of classical yoga philosophy.

THE EIGHT LIMBS OF YOGA: YOUR SPIRITUAL NAVIGATION SYSTEM

We'll start with the first two Limbs, the Yamas and Niyamas, and cover the others in a later chapter. The ancient Indian sage, mystic, and philosopher Patanjali didn't invent the Yamas (ethical guidelines for how we treat others and this world) and Niyamas (personal practices and observances that are the foundations of self-care), but he organized them into a structured system that became the basis for classical yoga. It's basically the ultimate self-help guide.

The Yamas: Your Guide to Getting Over Yourself and Being a Good Person

We all have, as the saying goes, a "wise guide inside." The Yamas, the first of yoga's Eight Limbs, inform that guide, serving as a template for how to interact with the world without being, well, a jerk. They're five universal rules to help you live a more compassionate life:

∞ **Ahimsa (non-violence, aka, don't be mean):** This is more than just not punching someone in the actual face. It's about non-violence in your actions, your words, and even your thoughts. It's the little voice inside that says, "Don't freak out and flip a bird or scream at the car that just cut you off in traffic." Ahimsa encourages you to be kind to everyone, including, and importantly, yourself. Find yourself in one of your negative thought loops? What would you tell a beloved friend about that? Ahimsa encourages conscious altering of the inner critic's nonsense: be kind to yourself, and then reflect that outward.

∞ **Satya (tell the truth):** Honesty is always super important, but here's the rub: it should always be balanced with Ahimsa. Speak your truth, but not if it's going to hurt someone needlessly in the process. So, be authentic, but maybe don't offer an unsolicited critique of your friend's new bag that's just… well, hideous. Keep that thought to yourself.

∞ **Asteya (don't steal stuff):** This one is pretty straightforward; I mean, it goes without saying, really. Don't take things that don't belong to you. But it also goes deeper than that. It means respecting other people's time, their energy, and their ideas. Basically, don't be a human vacuum cleaner. Don't suck.

∞ **Brahmacharya (use your energy wisely):** While this was originally about celibacy (no judgment), the modern take is about using your energy in a smart way. It's about finding a healthy balance in life and not wasting your time and potential. It's the reason you should probably stop binge-watching that show and instead feed your passion, learn something new, work on a project, or maybe start writing your unique and interesting story.

∞ **Aparigraha (let go of greed, aka non-attachment):** This is all about not chasing an ideal, gathering endless things, or being possessive, and instead learning to be content with what you have. It's the simple joy of not needing to buy something from every single ad that you see and finding peace in a life that's just enough. It's a practice of gratitude. It's a practice of letting go of what you don't need, both physically and emotionally. Ask yourself the question, "What no longer serves me?"—and let it go.

The Niyamas: Your Self-Care To-Do List

If the Yamas are about how you show up in the world, the Niyamas are about how you show up for yourself. They're five personal practices that are less about what you do and more about who you're becoming:

∞ **Saucha (clean up your act):** This is about more than just giving the living room a nice straightening up and dusting. Saucha refers to internal and external cleanliness. It's making sure your body is nourished and healthy, your mind isn't cluttered with negativity, and your work and home spaces aren't a total disaster area. A clear mind starts with a decluttered environment. It's the whole idea behind the minimalist movement. But you don't need to be a minimalist to clean out your body, mind, and spaces.

∞ **Santosha (be happy anyway):** This is the practice of finding contentment right where you are, and realizing that happiness isn't some destination you have to go find. It's remembering that there's a happy place inside, a little buoyant cork of joy, a part of you that's always happy, for no particular reason at all. It's thankfulness for where you are, what you have, the air in your lungs, the breeze on your skin, and the gift of life.

∞ **Tapas (get it!):** Tapas is the fire. It's stepping on the gas of self-discipline and applying effort. It's the inner drive that helps you identify then stick with your goals, even when you really just want to lie down and take a big nap. Think of it as the willpower to get on your mat even when your couch is calling your name, or to fire up that core in Crow Pose and fly!

∞ **Svadhyaya (get to know yourself):** This one is all about self-study and learning. It means looking inward to figure out what makes you tick. Self-awareness is more rare than you'd think. Taking an honest look and understanding what's important to you, and how you're processing the world and your experience of it, is work worth doing. We'll talk more about this when we get to our writing practice, as that's a key tool here.

∞ **Ishvara Pranidhana (just let go):** This means surrendering to something bigger than yourself, whether you call it the universe, a higher power, your higher self, or just a sense of purpose. It's releasing control and trusting that you're on the right path, even if it feels a little wobbly sometimes.

Beyond the foundational ethical principles of the first two Limbs—the Yamas and Niyamas—the Eight Limbs of Yoga provide a treasure trove of concepts that further illuminate the path to self-realization and inner peace. These teachings give us a framework for understanding the nature of existence, the workings of the mind, and the transformative power of a yoga practice. In the chapters that follow, we'll begin the work of applying that framework to our writing practice as well. The Yamas tell us how to show up in the world, the Niyamas tell us how to turn toward ourselves, and the remaining Limbs continue that inward path. We'll continue our walk down that path shortly.

PUT IT INTO PRACTICE

This exercise is an invitation to go beyond intellectual understanding and begin integrating these ancient principles into your daily life and your writing practice. I've chosen one of the Yamas for you, Ahimsa. Choose a second that you find relates most strongly to the work we're doing here in our *Ink & Asana* practice.

- ☐ **Ahimsa (non-violence):** In your journal, briefly define Ahimsa in your own words. What does "non-violence" mean to you in your daily interactions, your words, and even your thoughts toward others and yourself? How might you apply it to your writing practice? Think of one concrete way in which you can apply Ahimsa in your interactions today or this week.

- ☐ **Choose one more Yama (Satya, Asteya, Brahmacharya, or Aparigraha):**
  - ∞ Write down the name of the Yama you chose.
  - ∞ Define it in your own words.
  - ∞ Identify one specific action you can take to embody this Yama in your daily life or in your writing practice.

I've chosen Svadhyaya (self-study) as your first Niyama to work on below. Choose a second that you feel is most relevant to your personal growth right now, or that you'd like to cultivate more deeply.

- ☐ **Svadhyaya (self-study):**

    - ∞ In your journal, define Svadhyaya in your own words. How do you go about getting to know yourself?

    - ∞ This Niyama is particularly powerful for writers. Commit to one self-study writing practice this week. This could be five to seven minutes of free-writing about a recent emotion, exploring why you reacted a certain way to an event, or simply listing what you value most.

- ☐ **Choose one more Niyama (Saucha, Santosha, Tapas, or Ishvara Pranidhana):**

    - ∞ Write down the name of the Niyama you chose.

    - ∞ Define it in your own words.

    - ∞ Identify one specific action you can take to embody this Niyama in your daily life or in relation to your writing.

After completing the definitions and actions for each Yama and Niyama, take a few moments to sit with your reflections.

☐ How did it feel to articulate these ancient principles in your own context?

☐ Do you notice any immediate shifts in your perspective or motivation?

☐ Keep your journal handy throughout the week, revisiting your chosen Yamas and Niyamas as reminders and guides for your actions and your writing. We'll be exploring these even more deeply as we go forward.

02

HISTORY'S ECHO
The Wisdom of an Ancient Practice

In the wake of my mother's passing, I decided to take a trip to Key West by myself. She had been gone just a few months and I needed to spend some time there on my own. I couldn't really articulate exactly why, or what I intended to do there; I just needed to go. We'd spent so much time on that island—it was Mom's hometown and where we went many times every year. Grandma lived in the same house on Elizabeth Street for seventy years, until she too died, just twenty months before my mom.

We had been three; now I was one.

It was May, so the poinciana trees were blooming red all over the place. As I drove down the Keys, I felt sort of like I was going there to look for something. I was seeking, hoping to find something of… what, I didn't know. Because what I truly wanted was no longer there. I took little joy driving over the bridges and seeing my beloved, beautiful Keys water.

Key West looked as it always had, and yet, it had changed. In my hotel room—where it was weird to be in and of itself, since we'd always stayed at Grandma's house—I unpacked. Out of a tote bag, I pulled my mother's book: the history of our family, and the stories she'd compiled. I wanted to spend time with her work, her words.

Back when I was a kid, she'd started working on what would become her life's work. Seeing that her grandmother, my great-grandmother, was getting on in age, Mom wanted to write down all of her grandmother's stories and memories to preserve them for herself and us. Then she expanded that work and did the same for anyone else in the family willing to tell stories—and let me tell you, that was all of them. It's what they do, have always done. She wrote it all down, and began researching records and the family tree—and genealogy became her beloved hobby ever after.

It was through her work, her documentation, reflections, and research, that I was able to sit on the balcony of my hotel room and spend time with all of it when I needed to the most. She had given me the gift of her words, her legacy, and I was holding it all in my hands.

Far from being just a tool for communication, writing has been a sacred act, a therapeutic practice, and a vehicle for self-exploration since its earliest manifestations. It's inseparable from the human experience, as we've always been compelled to leave our mark on the world. From the careful chiseling of hieroglyphs on temple walls to the meticulous calligraphy in countless manuscripts, the act of putting thought into tangible form has always had a deeper significance than simply conveying information. Think of your own call to write. Doesn't it have the feel of instinct? Just as you may feel pulled to the mat, the urge to write is an ancient force within you. Feeling drawn to the craft, even if just to journal for yourself, has roots in all of human history.

Throughout the ages and in every culture, humans have turned to writing not just to make records of history, but to understand it. It has served as our way of working to understand ourselves and to connect both with each other and with something larger than us. We have long used writing to form communities, share thoughts and theories, and ensure legacy. The wisdom embedded in this instinctive and ancient practice offers important lessons for our own lives, particularly in an unprecedented age of digital noise and short attention spans.

Your desire to tell your story isn't an act of self-indulgence; it's your natural human instinct to leave a mark. When you ran into your neighbor at the grocery store last week and exchanged a little chit-chat to catch up, it may have turned into her discussing a friend who had an illness. Since you yourself have experience with that same illness, you felt compelled to tell her about some of the things that have helped you. Writing is the physical form of that same brand of kindness, as you document what you've learned in a way that will help your community. That's how humans care for each other. It's an offering.

Just as yoga helps us remember our inherent wholeness and peace, the practice of writing can serve as a powerful tool for this same kind of memory. Through the act of putting ink to page, whether paper or digital, we engage in a form of Svadhyaya. As we study our selves, our experiences, emotions, and past, writing allows us to dive below our conscious thoughts and self-talk, to reveal deeper truths and insights about who we truly are. It's a process of excavation, or digging, in a quest for the authentic self, remembering circumstances and motives that may have been forgotten or bringing maturity and understanding to the events experienced by younger selves.

The writer in me came to life as I was working on my memoir, and frankly, I'd always known she was there. I don't know how I knew. As the saying goes, "a writer writes," but I hadn't. For work, yes—training programs, processes and procedures—and I was drawn to creative roles, but this type of writing was a first. As I progressed through my project, that sense of "remembering" was persistent, just as it is in yoga. It wasn't instinct alone; it was also my family's history of storytelling, and that of humanity itself. My mother was a storyteller and a writer. Her legacy had awakened within me.

You can see how interconnected this can be with yoga, as both practices will complement and enhance the other's ability to provide such growth, ease, and wisdom. Both activities crack open human experience and offer expansive growth, but in different ways, complementing each other and forming a complete practice.

FROM RECORD-KEEPING TO REVELATION

Imagine you're a farmer in ancient Mesopotamia, circa 3200 B.C. We'll call you Bob. Farmer Bob. You grow grain, dates, maybe some flax here and there, and you're thinking about expanding into offering cooking oils to broaden your marketing appeal. You regularly trade your grain and dates for some Babylonian textiles. With the addition of cooking oils, it's becoming a lot to keep track of, and spreadsheets don't exist yet. So, Bob, you look around you and see your tools and some nearby clay. Forming a tablet out of the clay, you then press wedge-shaped marks into it to keep track of your growing farm business, your trades, and other transactions.

This is how writing started: with the pragmatic. The earliest forms of formal writing, showing up around Bob's time, were called cuneiform. They were wedge-shaped marks pressed into clay tablets, which served as an accounting system for agricultural surpluses and trade. This is one of the earliest forms of formal writing that we know of, but there were earlier forms still. Ancient Egyptian hieroglyphs, showing up around the same time and also serving administrative purposes at first, quickly branched into religious texts, inscriptions on monuments, and elaborate narratives that aimed to connect the living with the divine. This dual function was a precedent for writing's future. It was simultaneously a tool for everyday tasks and a pathway to the spiritual.

What can start as documentation can lead to revelation. That was true for all of humanity, from the pharaohs to Farmer Bob, and it's true now.

What can we learn from writing's origin? Well, first, the value of documentation. Even seemingly simple records—when preserved, become invaluable insights into past societies. My mom's genealogy research was full of little everyday records, logs, letters, deeds, birth and death certificates—all pieces of a big puzzle that would help her put together our history. Have you ever been to a history museum and marveled at the level of information available? And that's just the tip of the iceberg. If you haven't already done so, go to the Museum of Natural History in New York City—it will knock your socks clean off. The vast quantity of documentation by past societies gives us a window into their lives.

My mother loved all things documented. Records were her thing. Any genealogist will tell you how much they love spending time in dusty old libraries and archives, looking for that one clue that will answer a question that will connect the dots and prove a theory. All those little bits and pieces of information tell a story. And if we're lucky, someone in the family (like my mom) wrote those stories down.

As I sat on my Key West hotel room balcony, reading my mother's words, I was able to not just learn about what life was like for previous generations, but to read her interpretation of the events, and her impressions of the people, places, and conversations that had taken place. Her voice lives in her words. She had explored the past for us, excavating and organizing it for us. She was a wealth of information, always telling us stories throughout our lives; the amount of detail she knew off the top of her head was staggering, and I got to revisit it all after she was gone. How beautiful to spend time with her constant study, her labor of love.

That's the power of journaling, writing a memoir, or simply taking notes. The act of externalizing our thoughts, even if just for personal consumption, lends them a certain weight and clarity that unwritten thoughts often lack.

☐ Try this exercise. The next time you're frustrated with someone, and find yourself rehearsing a future conversation with them (a conversation that, let's face it, may never actually happen), stop talking to the mirror and instead write them a letter. You don't have to send it, and you shouldn't even write it as if you are going to send it. Write it as it's happening in your mind, as you point and bow up on that mirror of yours. Let it all go; get it out of you and onto the page. Then walk away from it for a couple of days. When those days have passed, return to your letter and read it. What do you think about it now? How has externalizing your swirling thoughts changed them?

Most humans are visual—sixty-five percent of us, actually. Seeing information in written form, even that which comes from within our own minds, enhances understanding, comprehension, and memory and allows for the expulsion of complex thoughts. It paves the way for detached observation, a crucial step in understanding our own inner workings.

I experienced this first-hand when I wrote my memoir. I began by writing letters to my mother, but that quickly turned into me documenting my memories and as much of our time together as I could. I did so for me, but also for my family, to create a record, a collective memory that would add to her legacy. The process of laying out those memories and facing down my past decisions, mistakes, and challenges started to change them. It's as if I was a third-party observer instead of an active participant, and that completely altered my perspective.

Beyond mere documentation, early writing quickly became a means of preserving wisdom and cultural identity. The great epic poems, legal codes, and religious texts of ancient civilizations weren't just stories, guidelines, or rules; they were the very fabric of their societies, painstakingly transcribed and passed down.

Writing is a legacy builder. What we choose to write and preserve, whether it's personal narratives or shared knowledge, becomes a part of the ongoing human story, a gift to future generations. This was my mother's motivation for her life's work in digging through the genealogy of our family—she believed we must understand where we came from if we are to have any hope of truly knowing ourselves.

The impulse to write a memoir, for example, is a modern echo of the ancient desire to document and share a unique experience, allowing it to resonate beyond one's lifetime. Think of what your story could do for those who read it, even if you help just one person reframe their experience or connect with yours.

WRITING AS A SPIRITUAL AND PHILOSOPHICAL DISCIPLINE

In many ancient traditions, writing was linked with spiritual and philosophical development. In India, the *Upanishads* and the *Yoga Sutras* of Patanjali were not just academic works but guides for self-realization. The act of composing, copying, and studying these texts was itself a meditative and transformative practice. Still is. In ancient China, calligraphy was considered a high art form, intimately connected to the principles of Taoism and Zen Buddhism. The discipline required to master the brush, the flow of ink, and the balance of characters mirrored the pursuit of inner harmony and enlightenment.

Writing is a practice, and a discipline for the mind. Just as yoga cultivates physical discipline, the act of writing cultivates mental discipline, Tapas. It demands focus, patience, and the ability to organize chaotic thoughts into coherent structures. And just like any practice, some days we're better at it than others. It's a practice of sustained attention, much like meditation. If you don't yet feel that sustained attention, still finding yourself sitting down to write and quickly noticing your attention drift elsewhere, don't worry; we'll address that. If you're already an avid writer, you're no doubt familiar with the "mad scientist" intensity that can compel an author to the keyboard every free second of the day. But even in times of flow, we can get stuck. Switching gears and turning from inspiration to discipline can get us right back to inspiration.

When we engage in free-writing or journaling, we are, in a sense, performing a mental asana: stretching our thoughts, holding them up for inspection, and gently releasing what no longer serves us. The very process of forming words, sentences, and paragraphs helps to untangle the knots of our minds, leading to greater clarity.

In school, we're all taught *how* to write, but I don't remember anyone really getting into *why*. It's all about self-discovery and introspection when we write about our own lives. This practice of "writing as a mirror" allows us to see our own thoughts and experiences externalized, enabling us to examine them with a degree of detachment and objectivity. It's a powerful way to process emotions, face fears, and articulate what we hold close and believe.

THE THERAPEUTIC POWER OF THE PEN

It wasn't until I was writing one of the last letters to my mother, at the end of my quest for answers about my health, that it dawned on me how much my perspective had changed. I realized how much more kindness I was now offering myself—about my past, about my illness. Now, I could easily see how I had beat myself up over the years. But as a detached (ish!) observer, I was able to see my story as someone else would. And the advice and grace I would give the author if they'd shared it with me? Well, that was profoundly different from the self-talk I had been engaging in for a very long time. My heart went out to the woman in those pages, and my eyes were opened.

I'd found a new way of framing every single part of my story. My health: I could see that it had actually declined ever so slowly over decades, not suddenly. My past missteps: I saw them now as decisions made from a place of love, not mistakes. My grief: I no longer thought of it as a burden to carry, or a cloud to be lifted—I now loved my grief and held it gently, feeling it was my honor to carry it. My own narrative—the stories I'd told myself—had changed. And that reframing wasn't something I did on purpose. I was shocked and delighted by it. And I felt lighter, brighter, like someone had switched the sun back on.

While no one called it "therapy," many ancient writing practices served a therapeutic function. For example, some of the inscriptions on ancient Egyptian tomb walls express deep grief and a desire for connection with the deceased. When the loss of someone you love is so very great, how do you express that without art, or without words written for others or the universe to see? An emotion so deeply felt, so immense, must be sent outward. That was, after all, exactly what I did. No one told me to do it; it was pure instinct. The act of committing these intense feelings to a permanent medium could have offered a form of release and processing for ancient cultures, similar to what I experienced when writing to my mother and exploring our time together.

The therapeutic value of writing transforms the act from a task or a project into a full expression of something you didn't know you had to say. Writing can be a way of putting your story through the wash, as I like to say, for that's what it felt like. It's a process of cleansing grief and trauma—not eliminating them, but transforming them, and therefore also transforming the author. It allows us to spew out all the things we're too afraid to talk about. Apologies for that visual, but that's what it can emotionally resemble.

By externalizing our pain, our fears, and our anxieties onto the page, we begin to take their power away. The act of writing a difficult memory, for instance, transforms it from an overwhelming internal sensation into a manageable narrative, allowing for reflection and reframing. This is definitely the case in memoir writing. It clears the clutter in the mind, and gets all that stuff organized so you can decide what to do with it.

Often, we think that memoirists had a story to tell that included their transformation, so they wrote it. But sometimes, the transformation happens through the writing. They tell their story, then how they see it changes, and then they revise the story with their new wisdom and perspective, holding it at arm's length and going, "Huh. Well, would you look at that?"

A CATALYST FOR CHANGE AND CONNECTION

My story contains a controversial topic, although frankly, it shouldn't be seen that way. But I acknowledge people have certain feelings about it—judgmental feelings that are a conversation, perhaps, for another day. In my own memoir, I decided to include a chapter about an experience that originally I wanted to keep private; however, the political climate of recent years, and an act of the Supreme Court in 2022, convinced me it was time to share it. The overturning of *Roe v. Wade* hit me hard. I decided to tell my story about how that law had once saved my life. I felt it was time to lift the veil of shame I'd carried for three decades and put it out there into the world. For I feel all stories like mine should be told if one feels compelled to do so. We are an army of survivors, and each story is unique and important. I hope that if enough stories are told, the tide will begin to turn once again.

In writing a memoir, you get to choose which parts of your life you will tell, and what you will keep private. If you're going to share your story with the world, you may wish to drum up your courage and tell a story that could spark understanding in those who don't currently possess it, move others to positive action, or give encouragement to those who need it.

Throughout history, writing has been a potent force for social and political change. From revolutionary manifestos to personal letters that inspired and mobilized movements, the written word has proposed action, challenged injustices, and united communities. There's a pile of impactful works that sparked revolutions, championed human rights, or simply articulated a collective aspiration for humanity. Today, that continues, although more than ever we have to be vigilant about vetting sources—as the misinformation machine is real. And these days, writing is often used to fuel support for ideas that can hurt factions of our society—and it's sometimes sadly hidden behind righteous or spiritual belief.

The more we can put our truth out there, with positive messaging, the more we serve something beyond ourselves, combatting false and misleading information with what's real: true human experience. Flood the zone with truth and love.

In a later chapter, we'll explore how writing can transform the helplessness one can feel in a polarized political climate, especially when rights are actively threatened and even removed. Our words can align us to stand together, but they can also serve as a way to step back and focus on what's going on inside, so that we can grow stronger and more peaceful. Only then can we turn outward to help others. Writing your fears and concerns can quickly turn to action, and a plan can come into focus—one that you can then use to make positive change, not only in your own life but in the lives of others.

Our stories, when shared, have the power to resonate with others, build empathy, and even inspire collective action. Whether it's a personal blog post, an essay, or a book, sharing our unique experiences and insights can foster understanding and belonging. It allows us to articulate our purpose and contribute to a larger conversation.

Your voice matters, so give the world the gift of it. The act of writing can move us beyond feeling powerless to taking small, meaningful steps toward positive change in the world.

Making a Mark

From the charcoal-etched walls of ancient civilizations to the delicate ink applied with feather quill pens, the human hand has always reached for a way to say: 'I was here. This mattered.' When you pick up your pen today, you are not just writing; you are joining a prehistoric lineage of witnesses. You are part of a continuous line, holding the power of the pen for a brief, beautiful moment before passing it into the hands of the future.

The Somatic Inquiry:
Hold your pen in your hand and close your eyes. Feel the weight of it. Before you write a single word, acknowledge that this tool is the bridge between your fleeting thoughts and your permanent legacy.

PUT IT INTO PRACTICE

In our increasingly online and screen-saturated lives, the ancient wisdom of writing is more relevant than ever. Try these yoga-inspired ways of working.

- ☐ **Cultivate presence.** Just as we roll out a mat in an uncluttered space, try creating a sacred space for writing and engaging in pre-writing rituals like mindful breathing. When journaling, sit in your quiet space, journal in your lap or on a table or desk in front of you. Get out your favorite pen. Sit in contemplation briefly before beginning. If using a computer, turn notifications off, clear your desk of items that don't serve you in this sacred space, and breathe deeply, letting inspiration flow through you. This grounds us in the moment, and allows us to unclutter our minds, free from digital distractions and the relentless pull of the external.

- ☐ **Embrace the process, not just the product.** Early writing was often practical and for documentation. Our writing, especially for self-discovery, benefits from a focus on the act itself, rather than solely on a polished final product. If it ends up a bestseller, great, but that's not our motive for taking to the keyboard. Embracing the mess, the imperfection, and the process as a sacred part of self-discovery allows genuine wisdom to emerge. It's the expression that matters, and there's no wrong way to do that.

☐ **Harness the therapeutic power of writing.** Utilize writing as a tool for emotional processing. Journaling, free-writing, and stream of consciousness can help navigate emotions, fears, and desires. Just as ancient drawings and carvings offered release, our writing can help us expel difficult emotions and take their power away.

☐ **Connect with legacy and purpose.** Whether writing a memoir, documenting a personal reflection, or working on a report, recognize the ancient impulse to leave a trace, to contribute to the human story. My mother was a storyteller, our family's genealogist. Her life's work was to compile not just our heritage but the stories from those who came before—to immortalize them and make sure that future generations understand where they came from and what informs their own lives. Your unique voice and perspective are valuable, and committing them to written form creates a lasting impact.

03

ASANA
The Story of the Body

The body is the way in. The ritual of stepping to the front of the mat, "arriving," centering the mind with an opening like bringing the hands together in front of the heart, palms touching to symbolically connect body and mind, is the entry point. Not every practice has to start that way, but for me, a lot of them do. Ritual can create an auto-response. Just by routinely incorporating certain acts or motions, your body instantly knows how to respond. Similar to Pavlov's dogs, who would salivate at the ringing of a bell, our inner puppy starts to wag its tail in anticipation of the incoming asana. Immediately, the breath slows, as we intentionally bring our focus there. The rest of the world starts to fall away. As we flow through the poses, we notice how we feel, and we work through the stories that are caught in our joints and muscles—even though we have no idea that's what we're doing at the time. It all happens automatically, just by starting the practice.

After my initiation into yoga through Yin, and once I began to heal, I started branching out. I learned Hatha and Ashtanga, but it was Vinyasa that really sang to me. The fluid movements were warming and opened me up, fueling my body's need for expansion and strength. My life raft had evolved into a sanctuary that I still retreated to daily, but now I varied what kind of yoga style I did based on how I felt each day.

It's a practice of mindfulness not just to notice how we feel in each pose and determine how we'll show up in flow, but also to notice how we feel before we even begin the practice, and make choices that nourish us, and meet us where we are.

Around the time I lost my grandmother, and then my mother, I again stumbled upon the teachings of a master. I found Blissology Yoga, founded by Eoin Finn, at a time when I wasn't sure how to be happy; my grief was swamping me. It was actually an online class called "Yoga for Happiness" that introduced Eoin's style to me. His easy way, and joyous cues made me smile, and I knew I'd want to take any class that he taught. Eoin's Blissology Yoga, with his own variations, creative flows, and intelligent somatics, became foundational to my practice—so much so that, years later, I became a certified yoga teacher by completing Eoin's teacher training program. It's not just the joy, or the flow state, or the fitness that's profound for me; it's the intelligent way of helping students figure out how to fit yoga poses to their bodies, not the other way around.

ASANA: THE POSTURES

This is usually the first thing everyone thinks of. And while often the most visible aspect of yoga in the Western world, asana is the third of the Eight Limbs. The physical poses are designed to purify the body and create stability, strength, and flexibility. They were actually created by the ancient yogis as a way to ensure they could sit in meditation for very long periods of time. Meditation, and ultimately, enlightenment by going within and creating total stillness was the real goal. But sitting for a long period of time can be difficult, unless the body is cared for in such a way that it allows you to do so. Releasing tension, and promoting a solid and flexible foundation to sit in, the yoga poses were originally the journey, not the destination. And so it should remain today, but unfortunately a great deal of focus is placed on reaching the "perfect" pose.

The advent of social media has brought us into a very visual world, which is contrary to yoga philosophy. The perfect splits, the deepest backbend, or having your thigh bones directly parallel to the ground in Warrior II have become the goal—all in the name of that beautiful Instagram pic. Often, cues to reach those "perfect" poses come in the name of "alignment," but I propose that "attunement," as in to tune into your body's needs, is far more important than lining bones up with other bones, the floor, or the wall.

I was lucky enough to find a teacher training program that focused on smart yoga: getting more out of the postures than a picture. As Eoin always says, "Yoga is a feeling, not a shape." Striving for some image of what you think a pose "should" look like is a surefire way to end up injured—and many of us have. We also do a disservice to the history and lineage that is yoga if we ignore the inner work while pursuing an unrealistic aesthetic. With asana as the gateway to real yoga, you have to actually get through the gateway safely to make it to the real work. Think of it this way: if you were trying to get into the best, most exciting and exclusive nightclub in the world, but on your way through the door, the bouncer just randomly kicked your ass as you tried to get in, you aren't likely to try to get into that nightclub again any time soon, am I right? Your teacher's job is to escort you around the ass-kicking bouncer so that you can get to the good stuff. Yoga teachers today must combat our visually obsessed culture by helping yoga students find their own version of a pose—one that works for their specific anatomy and body type—not some idealistic (and unrealistic) version of a shape. Once we do that, then the real work can begin.

This likely won't come as a shock, but all humans are different. We are all made as individuals, and while our bones and connective tissues are all similar, they're not exactly the same. My femur bone fits into my hip socket differently than yours. That directly impacts my ability to reach the "full expression" of a pose, as it does yours. For example, if a femur head is situated closer to the side of the pelvis, the leg may not be able to abduct (lift to the side) as much as it does for someone who naturally has more space there. When you have more space, it can look like more flexibility—so the person with the closer fit won't be able to do center splits as easily as the other person.

I'm one of those people, actually. I can do Hanumanasana (full splits) easily, because my bones are situated in a way that allows it. But Samakonasana, or center splits (legs out to the side)? Not so much. I get stuck way up off the ground. And I'm what you'd call a pretty flexible person. That's not to say that I can't work to make progress, but knowing that it's my bones that are stopping me is important, so I don't push too hard and end up injuring myself.

When we say, "Listen to your body," that's what we're talking about. Because of how my bones work together, I have to be satisfied with my version of the pose and not go too far. If I pay attention, I can feel that there's some work I can do to create space—just not too much.

Patanjali's foundational instruction for asana, **sthira sukham asanam**, translates to steadiness and effort (sthira) and ease (sukha) in posture (asana), but its wisdom extends far beyond the physical shape. It stresses the duality of **sthira** and **sukha**, urging students to find a dynamic balance within each pose. This duality, inherent in every asana, becomes a powerful metaphor for life itself, teaching us to navigate challenges with grounded resilience while finding moments of grace and surrender. Finding that balance, in practice and in life, pushes us to grow—but to do so with joy and ease.

The real beauty in the asana practice comes when we are able to make it our own, focusing on the feeling, not the shape. Alignment is important only in that we approach it in a consciously somatic way, fitting the pose to our bodies, not our bodies into the pose.

Most of us don't have the goal of sitting in meditation for long periods of time—although I would fully encourage you to incorporate meditation into your practice, as sitting in stillness and the art of watching thoughts go by are extraordinarily valuable skills. But even if we don't, the asana practice removes tension so that when we are in Savasana (final resting pose) at the end, as I described in the Introduction, clarity is reached, and we get to the real deal. My best ideas happen in Savasana, but also my clearest realizations. When tension is removed, we get to what's underneath, and that's a very healthy way to deal with trauma, sadness, grief, or even fatigue. Find out what's really going on, and only then can you truly start to make positive change.

THE BODY: SACRED TEMPLE OR TOOL?

How do you view the physical form you inhabit? In yoga, the body is often described with powerful metaphors that shape our relationship with it. Is it a sacred temple, a dwelling place for the divine, something to be honored, protected, and revered? This perspective offers us kindness, self-care, and a deep respect for balance. Or is the body a finely tuned instrument, a tool to be sharpened, strengthened, and made supple? This view emphasizes discipline, functional movement, and the body's capacity to be the vehicle for our journey. Neither metaphor is right or wrong. They offer different lenses through which to approach our practice and our life. Exploring both allows for a way to frame our own body image, the motivation behind our self-care practices and how we approach them, and the deep connection between the physical self and an inner spiritual life. It invites you to consider: what is your current relationship with your body, and how does your yoga practice influence that perception? Yoga is for every body. We are all so very different, and come in so many shapes and sizes; this is our opportunity to determine how we will show up for ourselves, taking care, physically and emotionally, of this one vessel we are given.

Presence within my physical being was yet another gift yoga gave me. My body had started failing me, leaving me sad and frustrated with it. I felt "defective." But the acceptance that yoga helped me cultivate was not only an acceptance of my condition; it was an invitation to understand. And I began to appreciate this one life, whatever it was going to be, because I had found a way of excavating joy from within, even in the midst of suffering. My asana practice was the gateway to all of that.

THE KEYS TO THE GATE

Yoga offers several practice styles, each offering a unique approach to physical poses, breathwork, and philosophical insights. Here's a look at some of the most common styles, their origins, who they're for, how they're taught, and their foundational philosophies. Keep in mind that there can be a lot of overlapping between styles, as fusion and creative sequencing is very common.

Hatha Yoga

Technically, all modern yoga is Hatha Yoga, as the others are descendants of the original form. In Sanskrit, the word Hatha refers to the sun and moon ("ha" = sun, "tha" = moon), representing balance within the body. Generally featuring a slower pace than Vinyasa and Ashtanga, but more of a flow than Yin or Restorative, Hatha Yoga offers a pace that allows you to focus on each pose, learning your particular needs for alignment (attunement).

Hatha Yoga is one of the oldest forms of yoga, with roots dating back to ancient India. The term "Hatha" itself generally refers to any yoga that involves physical poses. Today, it's considered a slower-paced practice that emphasizes foundational poses and alignment. So, if you see an ad for a Hatha Yoga class, expect one that's medium paced, focusing on the integrity of the poses. In modern yoga, Hatha classes typically involve holding individual poses for several breaths, with a focus on mindful breathing, moving at a slower pace than more dynamic styles like Vinyasa. The intention of Hatha Yoga remains to prepare the body and mind for meditation, balancing energy.

Hatha Yoga is suitable for beginners (as is any type of yoga when a teacher designs a class for beginners or all levels) and those looking for a slower-paced practice. It's also beneficial for individuals who want to explore the spiritual and philosophical aspects of yoga in a less physically demanding way.

Often, you may not see a class listed or advertised as Hatha; it may just be "Yoga for Easing Lower Back Pain", or "Yoga for [fill in the blank]." This is true for other styles of yoga as well. So, it's important to read the descriptions of classes if available to understand what to expect. The teacher may not reference Hatha at all, but if the description mentions pacing, you may be able to figure it out.

Ashtanga Yoga

For the power yogi, Ashtanga is about discipline, focus, and drive. That may seem counter to yoga's philosophies, but Ashtanga seeks to use the

Eight Limbs and other concepts to expand and purify the body and mind. Ashtanga Yoga was popularized by K. Pattabhi Jois in the 20th century, and is based on ancient texts and teachings. It's a highly structured and disciplined style of yoga. It's best for dedicated practitioners who thrive on routine and consistency, and are seeking a challenging physical and mental discipline. It's ideal for those who want to build significant strength, stamina, and focus.

Ashtanga follows a fixed sequence of poses, performed in the same order every time. It uses a specific breathing technique (Ujjayi breath) and Drishti (gaze points) to maintain focus. Classes can be led by a teacher or practiced "Mysore style," where students practice at their own pace with individual guidance.

Ashtanga aims to purify the body and mind through a rigorous and systematic practice. It follows Patanjali's Eight Limbs of Yoga, with a strong emphasis on self-discipline (Tapas) and concentration (Dharana) to achieve self-realization.

Yin Yoga

Ah, Yin Yoga. While I most often practice and teach Vinyasa and Hatha Yoga, I always incorporate Yin practices into my lineup. A big part of my heart is inhabited by Yin—it was where I began after all, and during such a difficult time. Yin classes were my life raft, in terribly turbulent seas, and they were my way into yoga.

A Yin class can consist of just a handful of poses, long-held and deeply opening. Even so, they can cause a powerful shift and be incredibly nourishing. The effects of Yin were so strong for me, I eventually became certified by Bernie Clark to teach Yin Yoga. It was not only foundational in my learning about the nervous system, but also yoga-specific anatomy and how Yin Yoga can benefit the body. Sip your cup of Yin slowly, and savor every drop.

Yin Yoga is a modern style developed in the late 1970s by Paulie Zink and later popularized by Paul Grilley and Bernie Clark. Yin draws inspiration from ancient Chinese Taoist practices and traditional Chinese medicine. It's often referred to as the "other half" to more active (yang) yoga styles. Working connective tissues and joints, Yin Yoga completes your fully rounded yoga practice, as the other forms are more focused on lengthening and strengthening the muscles.

This style emphasizes stillness, introspection, and patience, encouraging students to cultivate mindfulness and surrender to the sensations in the body. Bernie Clark highlights the science behind the poses and how deep breathing activates the parasympathetic nervous system. The effect is educational, while also deeply relaxing.

Yin Yoga is ideal for individuals seeking deep relaxation, increased flexibility, and release of tension in connective tissues. It's especially beneficial for those with stiff joints, or those who participate in more active forms of exercise, and can help activate the parasympathetic nervous system. The older we get, the more Yin Yoga becomes important, aiding mobility and ease.

Classes involve holding poses for extended periods, typically three to five minutes or even longer, primarily on the floor. Yin Yoga targets the deeper connective tissues of the body, such as ligaments, tendons, and fascia. To work these tissues effectively, long, static poses are necessary.

Yin Yoga aims to activate the parasympathetic nervous system, also known as the "rest and digest" system. This system promotes a state of calm and restoration, lowering heart rate, decreasing blood pressure, and directing energy toward vital functions like digestion and tissue repair. The conscious control of breathing, particularly with a longer exhale, sends signals to the brain to activate the parasympathetic nervous system, shifting the body from a "fight or flight" mode to a state of deep relaxation. The practice can lead to automatic calming through breath in daily life.

Vinyasa Yoga

Vinyasa is where yoga becomes a dance. It's a moving meditation. Linking breath and movement, a great deal of creativity can be woven in by each teacher's unique ways of doing so. Pace, content, and sequences can vary greatly, each teacher bringing their own flair to the practice. Even within the same teacher's classes, students may notice the freshness of each flow, as the Vinyasa style lends itself to creativity and finding unique variations and sequences. Blending tradition with modern takes on embodiment, Vinyasa is a yummy addition to your practice.

Vinyasa Yoga developed from Ashtanga yoga in the 20th century, becoming popular for its dynamic and flowing sequences. It's great for those who enjoy a more dynamic and fluid practice, seeking to build strength, flexibility, and cardiovascular health, while reaping the benefits to the mind. Some Vinyasa classes can be strong and include movements that strengthen the glutes, core stabilizers, abdominals, and inner thighs. Other Vinyasa classes can be slower, but fluid, combining a medium pace with mindfulness.

Vinyasa classes link breath with movement, flowing seamlessly from one pose to the next. The intention of Vinyasa is to create a meditative experience through continuous movement and breath. Vinyasa is a flow, whereby the mind becomes fully absorbed in the present moment, where we can embody peace.

Chair Yoga

Chair Yoga is for every body. It is a gentle, accessible form of yoga that is practiced while seated or using a chair for balance. It's ideal for anyone who prefers a gentle flow, is an office worker, has mobility limitations, or isn't interested in getting down onto a mat on the floor. Variations of traditional poses are cued, and just like other forms of yoga, Chair Yoga classes can be gentle and relaxing, as well as help build strength and flexibility.

Gentle chair-based poses stretch the muscles and improve joint range of motion. They provide stability, promote relaxation, and help manage chronic pain. It's important here to choose the right chair, using a stable, armless chair without wheels.

In Chair Yoga, we remove the distraction of balance and the effort caused by gravity. This creates ease, allowing the practitioner to turn their full attention inward toward breath and the stories living in the body.

Some classes are taught in tandem with other forms of yoga, with the teacher giving cues for both mat-based and chair-based yogis. This can serve as a powerful bridge between generations. It allows, for example, a mother and daughter to move in tandem, face-to-face, in a shared presence. It levels the field so the focus remains on the practice and on the connection. It also offers the opportunity for everyone to participate in the somatic writing practice outlined in this book. The benefits of going in and through the body to extract stories, memories, and transformation, are equal no matter which kind of yoga is practiced.

Restorative Yoga

When your body needs pure rest—if you're injured, emotionally drained, recovering from illness, or just want to relax as deeply as you can—find a Restorative Yoga class and get ready to go deep.

Restorative Yoga was developed by B.K.S. Iyengar, who emphasized the use of props to support the body in poses. It's perfect for anyone needing deep relaxation and gentle healing. It's especially beneficial for those recovering from illness or injury, feeling burned out,, or seeking to calm their nervous system.

Restorative classes use an abundance of props like blankets, bolsters, and blocks to fully support the body in comfortable, passive poses. Poses are held for an extended time, allowing for deep relaxation and release. It's deeply sedative, often taught with candlelight and soft music.

I obviously have my favorites, but I am just me, and you are you. I encourage you to find your own favorites by exploring each style that you're interested in. Just as we all have to find how poses fit our bodies, we need to find the style(s) of yoga that best fit our intentions, goals, and needs. Each style offers something unique—and every style can be integrated into your practice, if that's what feels right. You can choose just one, two, or possibly more. There's no right answer; it's just about what speaks to you.

Beyond the physical shapes and the immediate sensations, the yoga mat offers a unique and invaluable opportunity for self-study and experimentation. It serves as a safe refuge, a dedicated space where you can consciously observe your own patterns, habits, and reactions without judgment. This intentional self-observation is the essence of Svadhyaya, the yogic limb of self-study.

When you step onto your mat, and especially as you encounter challenging poses, your asana practice becomes a mirror reflecting what's going on inside. In a moment of physical discomfort or mental resistance, how do you speak to yourself? Does your inner critic chime in with discouraging remarks, or do you offer words of encouragement and compassion? Do you find yourself automatically pushing through pain, ignoring your body's clear signals, or do you pause, listen, and find a gentler way of talking to yourself?

Perhaps you notice a subtle urge to compare your pose to that of the person next to you, revealing tendencies toward competition or self-criticism. Or, you might observe a deep sense of resilience you didn't know you had.

The way you approach a difficult balancing pose, the way you respond to a prolonged stretch, or the thoughts that arise when you're still in Savasana—all of these moments offer insights into your default responses, your inner dialogue, and the influence of your ego. Here, we learn not to judge these patterns as "good" or "bad" but simply to witness them with curiosity. This is where the philosophical concept of Svadhyaya becomes tangible, a lived experience that extends far beyond ancient texts.

Remember, the goal in asana is not the perfect shape. What we're looking for is the feeling and an honest conversation with your body. By fitting the pose to your unique anatomy, listening deeply to your internal sensations, and understanding the subtle energetic shifts, you transform a physical exercise into a moving meditation and a living reflection of your inner life. This practice allows you to release tension, cultivate presence, and, ultimately, access the wisdom that lies beneath the surface.

As you continue to step onto your mat, let your asana practice be a continuous exploration, a safe space to move, breathe, and simply *be*. Allow the physical gateway to lead you deeper into your authentic self, cultivating the strength, flexibility, and inner peace that will serve you not only in your yoga, but in every moment of your writing and your life, on and off the mat.

The Body is an Archive

Your body is the first edition of your autobiography. Every joy, every grief, every season of struggle or triumph, has left it's "mark" in your body's tissues. They reside in the tension of your shoulders, the curve of your spine, and the strength in your hands. When we practice asana, we aren't just stretching the muscles. We are actually flipping through the pages of our own physical history. To move mindfully and with self-care is to honor the very vessel that has carried your entire life's history.

The Somatic Inquiry:
Close your eyes. Scan your body slowly, from the bottoms of your feet, all the way up to the crown of your head. Pause when you notice where a story might be stuck. Imagine your breath is an soft light illuminating a memory, a stress, or a feeling in a muscle or a joint. No need to correct it, just observe and breathe into it.

PUT IT INTO PRACTICE

Just as your yoga practice is a space for self-observation, your writing practice offers a complementary mirror, that allows you to articulate and process these insights. Take a few moments after your next asana practice to explore what you noticed during class:

☐ During [select a pose], what thoughts or emotions arose when I felt challenged? How did I speak to myself? Was my inner voice kind, critical, or neutral?

☐ In what ways did I compare myself to others in my practice today, if at all? What did that comparison reveal about my own expectations or insecurities?

☐ Describe a moment in your practice where you felt the perfect balance of effort (sthira) and ease (sukha). What did that feel like internally, both physically and mentally?

☐ What am I motivated by in my yoga practice? What are my goals?

☐ What do I want to embody, and learn more about? What specific asanas can support that?

☐ What cues can I incorporate to experiment and find the right pose modifications for my body?

☐ In which poses can I be kinder and more sustainable toward myself when I'm practicing?

☐ How can I give myself more grace, more forgiveness?

04

THE INNER DIALOGUE

Writing as a Mirror

When I sat down to write my first letter to my mother, after starting the process of making myself intentionally ill in the name of diagnosis, I had no idea I was going to write a book. I mean, I won't lie, I'd often thought about writing something over the years, and even thought I might one day write one about my mom and me, but this wasn't the moment I expected to begin. I simply wanted to feel her near me during a terrifying time, so I awkwardly wrote a letter telling her what was going on with me, and asking for her help.

It was a warm September Saturday morning when I sat down at my desk. I situated myself in the little nook I'd created in my yoga room. A small bedroom on the second floor of my home, my yoga room was my retreat from the world. Walls painted a cool light green, plants in the corners, and a closet repurposed as a place for my laptop, monitor, mouse, and keyboard to rest (and hide when I was filming yoga class videos).

I wrote that I needed her wisdom and calm presence, and then I added, "No, don't roll your eyes at the compliment; I'm serious." And that's when it became a dialogue. The more I wrote, the more I heard our conversation in my heart, and it came out onto the page. Memories started becoming more vivid—I could see them as clearly as I'm looking at these words as they fly across the screen right now.

I opened Jamboard (a now discontinued whiteboard-like app) that had a sticky note feature. I didn't know what order to put my memories in yet, because they were just popping up all over the place. So, I began by putting each "scene" on a sticky note. They were out of order and random at first, but as I started to think through them, I could see patterns forming. That was when it started to look like a book, but I'd hardly written anything beyond journal entries at this point.

The prospect of writing a book and possibly putting it out into the world made me physically nauseous. I vowed that it would be just for me. But after a while, I decided it would be for my niece and nephew as well. They were twelve and nine when my mom died, and didn't get nearly enough time with her. I was so very lucky to have her for the forty-one years that I did, and I would give them my memories—descriptive, vivid—and hope that they would one day give them a way to spend time with her as well. Storytelling is our family's love language; it was certainly my mom's, and now I would make it mine. She believed that we have to know and understand all the generations before us, to truly understand ourselves.

I was all aflutter, excited but a bundle of nerves. It was time to get onto the mat. The memories I wanted to write about were all a jumble in my mind. I needed to switch my brain off.

When you practice regularly, the mind can just click to the off position—and by that I don't mean all thought disappears, but there's a definite transition as soon as your feet settle in at the front of the mat. A big breath in, a big breath out. Time to flow and just let go. My teacher, Eoin Finn was on my monitor, taking me through the poses, the breathing, the finding of embodied peace. I flowed through my practice and, by the end, I felt more ready to sit in front of my sticky notes, brainstorm, start a journal entry, and breathe to let my memories and thoughts start to flow through me.

Memoir happens when journal entries start to turn into narrative, when what you've written for yourself gets repurposed and revised to potentially face outward and share your story with the world. Both journaling and memoir are the types of writing we're focusing on in this book, as they're powerful tools of self-discovery. But, obviously, I'm a big fan of non-fiction as well—that's when the rubber hits the road, and you turn that self-discovery and knowledge into tools and techniques you can share with others.

I'm not saying you have to do any of that. You may begin a deep journaling practice and decide that's all you want out of your writing life. It's for you and you alone, and that's beautiful.

A few days later, as I sat staring at my notes, my eyes kept floating over to one in particular, and I knew it would be my first chapter. It was a memory of a walk my mom and I took at the peak of my symptoms. It would be a difficult scene to tackle, as it was a time I had no desire to revisit. But I knew that if I was going to tell our stories, this one was not only representative of how she used to care for me, but also the reason I was going through the challenge of eating foods that would, over the next several weeks, start to give me pain. I dove straight into that difficult chapter as if I knew what I was doing (I didn't).

The first draft of that chapter was a stream of consciousness—a freewriting session that let the memory just burst out of me. I brought it out from the depths of my mind and just let it fly out onto the page. I typed and typed and got it out.

And there it was. I'd written a chapter. It wasn't terribly good, but that didn't matter. I'd done the work of setting it free.

And that was the first step.

PUTTING YOUR STORY THROUGH THE WASH

Writing is more than a communication tool or method of documentation. It's a profound practice of listening to yourself. It gives form to the formless, turning chaotic thoughts and feelings into something tangible and manageable. I had no idea any of that was possible, until I was almost done writing my story.

As I was worked through the rough draft and mentally regurgitated all of the memories I wanted to include, it started to take the form of a book, framed around the letters to my mother. I was at the end of my dietary challenge: many of my symptoms had returned. I had learned a lot and had a good understanding of what direction to take next with my health. I'd visited some painful memories and "mistakes" I'd made in the past. I'd spent time with the emotions I'd assigned to those days, and dove straight back into my trauma—several forms of it. I'd not just come face to face with my illness or my grief; I'd seen myself in a way I never had before.

And lightbulbs were going off. I was practically a lightbulb-producing machine, connecting dots, lifting the fog, and mixing metaphors all over the place. Holding up the mirror by writing my story, changed the story, and it changed how I felt about it. It was as if the story had been cleansed, and I was made free of it. This miraculous effect made me realize the mirroring effect of writing: not only how it shows us our reflection, but how that reflection starts to change.

THE MIRROR EFFECT

In the practice of yoga, we sometimes use a mirror not just to check our form, but to witness ourselves. The mirror reflects a truth you might otherwise ignore: the slight lift of a shoulder, the tension in your jaw, the way your breath hitches as you deepen a stretch. The mirror is a tool for self-observation, a way to see the person inhabiting the pose without judgment. You're there not to criticize, but to acknowledge.

When I was newer to yoga, I bought a big mirror, placed it in my yoga room, and used it as a guide. The longer I practiced, the more I realized that alignment must be felt, not created visually. So, while I see both yoga and writing as mirrors, the use of an actual physical mirror should be approached with caution. As we discussed in the previous chapter, never let the visual replace the somatic, as you feel your way into each pose. Yoga asana will reflect ourselves back to ourselves, by inviting us to honestly assess how we approach the practice and the poses.

The blank page is no different. It's the most honest mirror you'll ever encounter.

I first discovered this when I found myself trying to describe a day at the height of my illness, when my mother and I went for a walk at a wetlands park, a nearby nature center. I was aiming for a passage full of beauty and nostalgia, a loving tribute to my mom and how she walked me through the worst of times. But as I wrote about my illness and how it had taken hold, a different energy came through. Instead of sounding graceful, the words came across as brittle. I found myself using sharp, clipped sentences. "I was miserable." "Hopelessness was creeping in."

When I reread the passage, I saw something I hadn't realized I was feeling. The mirror of the page wasn't reflecting the beauty of the nature around us or the loving relationship between a mother and daughter; it was reflecting my own unspoken anger and grief. The words weren't describing the beauty of the day as much as they were about me feeling choked and overwhelmed by the memory of the worst of my illness. It was about how that memory existed in my mind, with the emotions I had attached to it since, rather than the day itself. And while I wanted to convey some of that, I also wanted the scene to show the contrast between natural beauty, the love and care my mom provided, and my fragile and broken body that was the victim of the situation. The chapter was coming across as ugly and gray, and I seemed bitter and closed off.

This is the **mirror effect** of writing. We sit down to write about a person, a place, or an event, but what emerges is an unvarnished reflection of our own emotions as they are today. Confronting how we feel or uncomfortable memories can shift perspective or release pent-up feelings, perhaps even forcing us to suddenly realize something we've never thought of before. We think we're writing about events, but in the end, we're always writing about ourselves. Our words are a perfect record of our current inner state.

This is why you must approach the blank page with the same non-judgmental curiosity you bring to a yoga practice. The reflection can be confronting. You might see a version of yourself you'd rather not acknowledge: the person who still carries resentment, who's clinging to old pain, or who feels a sense of inadequacy. The temptation is to look away, to close the laptop, to abandon the page.

Facing your emotions about a memory can be tough, so proceed with caution and take good care of yourself as you go. Take breaks, go for a walk, or pick it up again tomorrow. It took me some time to get through some of the more difficult recollections, but over time, getting in them and rolling around like a dog in a puddle made me wear them differently. I walked back into the world like that muddy dog, a goofy smile on my face, going, "Look what I got on me!" Those memories still aren't pleasant—it's still mud—but they're mine, and I started owning the hell out of them instead of letting them own me. I was no longer intimidated by them. I'd started to take my power back.

Just as a yoga mirror or close attention to sensation reveals where your body holds tension, the page reveals where your mind holds judgment or fear. Your first job is not to fix it but to **witness** it. The insight is the gift. In yoga, you don't instantly correct your posture; you first notice it. You attune to the way you want to move into the pose, and notice the difference between that and your current form. The same is true on the page.

As I edited my chapter, I realized it was time for me to go *into* the scene. To really *be* there and walk the walk. I started writing about stepping out of the car, feeling a curl of hair gently touch my forehead in the breeze, then drinking in the smells and sights of the sun-dappled wooden walkway. I wrote about my mother's way of walking, and how I wrapped my arms around my tight and painful abdomen. I saw the trees, the wind moving the palm fronds. I heard the moorhens and their crazy cackle. I heard my mother's voice. The image lifted, and I saw the beauty I was trying to get across. The memory became more vivid, and I felt immense gratitude—not just the pain of the memory. I realized that day was actually a turning point, not just a low point.

I had externalized my internal struggle by stepping away from it, and recreating a scene from the past. Now I'd created distance that allowed me to be more objective about my experience.

By acknowledging the reflection without turning away from it, you take the first step toward true clarity. You create the space for change. Your story is the image in the mirror, but the reflection is you. The more you write, the clearer the reflection becomes, and the more you learn about the beautiful, complex, and kick-ass fighter living within the pages, turning into someone who'll be the same but different on the other side of the completed work.

Transformation doesn't happen instantly. It takes time and many revisions, visiting with your memories and working through the steps. Your writing mirror is always there, ready to show you what you need to see. Approach it with the same curiosity, compassion, and courage you bring to your mat, and watch how your story, and your relationship to it, transforms.

Silvered Glass

When you write, the version of you that is constant stands before you. The reflection that we see in a physical mirror will consistently change over time, but the inner reflection writing provides is the purest form of you. The world would have us keep our focus on just the outside. But there is a wise guide inside. It is a voice that is often quiet, giving us cues in whispers so soft that we may miss them. Writing turns up the volume and lights the way.

The Somatic Inquiry:

Place one hand on your forehead, and one on your heart. Notice the temperature difference. Which engine is running hotter right now? Bring your hands in front of your heart and as you inhale let them float apart, palms soft. As you exhale, draw them together. Continue breathing this way, and as you do, imagine your heart expanding and filling with all of the wisdom you've inherited.

PUT IT INTO PRACTICE

Create your mirroring ritual. Let's build upon the pre-writing ritual we introduced to our writing practice in Chapter 2. Just as you might set up your yoga mat or space, create a conscious ritual before you write. That "clicking" that happens when you step onto the mat and take certain actions or movements? Give that to yourself in your writing practice.

- ☐ **Take a deep, clearing breath.** Take three deep, slow breaths, envisioning each exhale releasing expectation and judgment. This signals to your mind that this writing session is for honest self-reflection. Inhale inspiration. Exhale expectation.

- ☐ **Enjoy a moment of intention.** Before touching the pen or keyboard, briefly state, to yourself or aloud, your intention: "I'm writing today to vanquish some head trash about a painful memory," or "I'm writing to explore what I want to do as a next step in my career."

- ☐ **Use a sensory anchor.** Light a candle (I prefer flameless myself!), have a specific scent nearby, or play soft instrumental music. Music can remove inhibitions and really help you let go. Associate these sensory cues with your safe writing space.

Practice mirror writing, and witnessing without judgment:

- ☐ **The first pass.** This is about writing, not good writing. When tackling a memory or emotion, embrace the "free-writing" concept. Write without censoring. Don't worry if it's "good" or "ugly"—just get it out. This is your raw reflection.

- ☐ **Observe your emotions.** As you reread your fresh writing, notice what emotions emerge. Did a passage about a past event evoke anger you didn't realize was there? Did describing a challenge surface a surprising sense of "I don't actually care"? Simply *notice* these feelings, like observing a sensation in a yoga pose.

- ☐ **Identify your inner critic's voice.** When thoughts like "This is stupid" or "No one will want to read this" arise, acknowledge them. "Ah, there's my inner critic. You nasty little snot." Don't engage in a debate; simply let the thought float by, like a cloud. Return your focus to the words and your purpose.

Lean into the mirror effect for clarity and release:

- ☐ **Have a dialogue with what you wrote.** When a passage feels particularly loaded or reveals an uncomfortable truth, try writing a direct response to it. For example, if you wrote, "I felt like a victim," you might then write, "What does the victim version of me need to say right now?" or "What would the empowered, kick-ass version of me say about this moment?"

- ☐ **Reframe it with intention.** Once you've witnessed an uncomfortable truth, you have the power to reframe it. Like editing a photo to bring out its true colors, you can gently revise a section to reflect a newfound perspective. For instance, transforming "It was a low point" into "It was a turning point that taught me I had more strength than I knew." This isn't about denial, but about integrating the experience into a more empowering narrative, just as you might adjust a pose to feel sthira-sukha.

- ☐ **Put your story through the wash.** Revisit difficult memories or themes over time, by going through the revision process. Each time you read about them, and adjust your phrasing, tweaking this and that, it's another "wash cycle," subtly altering their emotional residue and allowing for deeper understanding and integration. The goal isn't to erase the past, but to transform its hold on you.

05

FINDING PRESENCE
The Power of Mindfulness

Think of this chapter as the secret sauce of yoga—the oh so yummy ingredient that's the path to peace. Mindfulness is a practice that can shift your perspective from "Oh no, another freakin' meeting" to "No worries, I've SO got this."

THE ART OF NOTICING, WITHOUT JUDGMENT

Here, we'll explore how to stop your brain from running a constant marathon of to-do lists and worries. Mindfulness teaches us to pay attention, moment by moment, without getting snagged by the silly stuff. This is where you practice being an observer of your thoughts, not their hostage.

In yogic philosophy, **citta vrittis** refers to the "fluctuations or modifications of the mind-stuff." Often translated as "turbulent thoughts," these are the constant whirlings and distractions of consciousness that prevent us from experiencing true stillness and clarity.

Think of the mind (citta) as a lake. When the wind blows across it, the surface becomes disturbed with ripples and waves (vrittis). In this turbulent state, you can't see the bottom of the lake clearly. The reflection on the surface is distorted. Similarly, when our mind is agitated by a continuous stream of thoughts, emotions, memories, and sensory input, our true nature—which is inherently peaceful and clear—becomes obscured. We have to train ourselves to sink beneath the waves of our turbulent thoughts.

These thoughts can manifest as misconceptions, or false understanding. This is when our perceptions are clouded by our own bias or incomplete information. Have you ever found yourself assuming what others are thinking, or imagining their true motivations without actually discussing it with them?

They can also arise as conceptualization or imagination. Worrying about a future event is actually a collection of thoughts not necessarily based on direct experience, but instead are imaginings of what might happen. You may find yourself running scenarios in anticipation of conversations or situations that haven't happened,or may never happen; this is a survival instinct for dangerous situations and has its uses, but we can consciously recognize when our mind is tapping into this tendency but isn't serving us by doing so. A great trick my mother taught me is to imagine a stop sign whenever you notice these kinds of thoughts.

And of course, citta vrittis may show up as memories, but the kind where we find ourselves ruminating on past events—whether pleasant or painful—which pulls us away from the present. And while we want to tap into some of this for the purposes of our writing, what I'm referring to here is more when you relive conversations over and over again, wishing you'd said something different, or when you rehash the past in an endless loop. We've all done it.

The practice of yoga, particularly through mindful asana, pranayama, and meditation, aims for **citta vritti nirodhah**—the calming of these fluctuations. By quieting the turbulent thoughts, the lake of the mind becomes still, allowing us to see our true reflection and experience the inherent peace and wisdom that lies beneath the surface.

For this very reason, I keep the image of a whale, in the form of a piece of wall art made of wood, in my yoga room. It's my reminder to sink beneath the turbulent waves of my thoughts, and find the stillness underneath.

That sinking may seem like it's easier said than done, but with practice it becomes natural. Turbulent thoughts are a part of life. You may find yourself with circular thoughts: loops of ideas that keep running through your head. If you have trouble sleeping, you've likely tried coaching the hell out of yourself. You know what I'm talking about, and I'm right there with you; I've done it a bazillion times:

Just breathe deep. Okay, good, slower. We're fine, everything is fine. I don't need sleep, I'm fine. Totally good here. If I sleep, good. If I don't, that's okay too. Six hours until my alarm goes off. Okay, that's fine. I'm fine. Sleeping is optional really, and I've powered through before. I may be a little tired tomorrow, but that's okay. Oops, forgot to breathe deeply, I should go back to that. Deep inhale, and let it out. That meeting tomorrow isn't that important anyway. I did some preparation, hopefully it was enough. The other people that will be in that meeting, they can cover for me, worst case scenario. I wonder if they ever have trouble sleeping? I'm sure they do, I mean, everyone does, right? Did I feed the cats? I think I hear one eating now, so that's fine. She's so cute, she was rolling on her back earlier, I should have taken a picture. My phone camera is really good—they've really made some amazing advances with technology. I should take more pictures and post them—I'm not active enough on social media. But social media is pretty toxic anyway, and the constant news posts are stressing me out. No wonder I can't sleep. Okay, breathe deeply. I'm fine. I'll be fine. Five hours and fifty-eight minutes to go, that's plenty.

If that, my friend, was at all familiar, you need mindfulness in your life. We'll talk about the breathing thing later, because it's absolute magic. The yogi's superpower is to calm racing thoughts and chill out. Mindfulness is the ability to observe thoughts—observe them passively—without judgement. No doubt when you were reading those thoughts above, you felt a little stressed out at the familiarity of it. You may have judged them as "bad," "unnecessary," "unavoidable," or just plain "nuts." It's okay; I can take it. But thoughts are natural—it's the mind's job to create thoughts. When we assign value or judge thoughts as "good" or "bad," we may get into trouble, because that judgement causes emotion. When we feel something about a thought, the emotion compounds it into more thoughts—and suddenly not only thinking, we're stressed, and then we get stressed about being stressed.

All of that, in addition to your natural emotions, feelings, and tension, gets stuck in the body, mired in your muscles and connective tissues. The asana practice works that out—when the issues are released from the tissues, as the saying goes, we're primed for true relaxation.

But the physical practice, as we learned earlier, is just one piece of the puzzle. Mindfulness is passive participation in the world around us, and the world within us. Focusing our attention on an object, event, or thought as a casual observer, without letting it create emotion, releases any control it may have over us. Mindfully watching a thought, or feeling the power and effects of asana, creates space for creativity and art.

Mindfulness is never about perfection. Just the opposite; it's about observation, and it's about practice. By weaving small moments of awareness into your day, you can build a strong foundation for a calmer, more focused life, and, ultimately, a more inspired and less stressful writing journey.

You'll notice that the "Put It into Practice" section that follows is longer than the others, with lots of ways to work mindfulness into your day. Take some time with it, to think about how you can make it a reality in your own life.

PUT IT INTO PRACTICE

A great way to get started with a mindfulness practice is to give yourself a retreat day. Dedicate a day to get into the here and now, and stay away from screens. Journal, write, and just unplug. Nourish your body with the most nutrient-dense fruits and vegetables, make soups and smoothies, and stay close to your food by preparing it yourself. Practice yoga. Meditate. A retreat day can be a boost to get your mindfulness going. Whether you start with a retreat day or not, here are some ways to work mindfulness into daily life.

Morning

☐ **Mindful waking.** Instead of grabbing your phone, take a few moments to simply notice your surroundings and the sensations in your body. I love this moment—you may already do this on weekend mornings, so it may seem familiar. You've woken up to sunlight peeking in around the sides of the closed blinds instead of to the alarm. Instinctively, you take a deep breath and stretch. Your eyes slowly open, and then close again. Before your to-do list creeps in, you assess how you feel, delighting in the potential the new day brings. But what about those weekdays when it's the blaring alarm that wakes you? First, do yourself a favor and select an alarm that wakes you up with a pleasant sound or music. Next, don't hit the snooze button; instead, turn the alarm off. Take a deep breath in and stretch from head to toe. Let the breath out, and take note of your toes and the rest of your body, all the way back up to the top of your head. No judgment about how you feel; just notice. Maybe notice the corners of your lips curling ever so slightly up toward your eyes in a little smile knowing (or deciding) that this is going to be a good day.

☐ **Conscious coffee or tea.** Pay attention to the aroma, the warmth of the mug, and the taste of each sip. Hold the mug in both hands, letting it warm your palms. Avoid distractions like the news. Instead of the couch, maybe park yourself at your kitchen table or in a chair by a window. Resist the pull of screens. Open your journal, and set your pen on top. Enjoy your cup of yum, breathing in the steam. Watch the sunrise, or write your day's intention. Emails, social media, news, can all wait. Especially if you're practicing mindfulness to foster creativity, don't kill it with to-do lists and technology. Instead, let it grow and blossom within you while your mind is fresh and clear. Everything else can wait.

☐ **Mindful movement.** Stretch your body slowly, noticing how each muscle feels. Whether you practice yoga in the morning or just do five minutes of stretching, this is your opportunity to create space in your body first thing in the morning, setting the tone for the entire day. Paying attention to how you feel in each movement, intuitively move in the way your body needs.

During the Day

☐ **Check in with all five of your senses.** Throughout the day, pause and identify one thing you can see, hear, smell, touch, and taste. This simple act brings you back to the present. This step was critical for me when managing the peak of my symptoms. The stress response that would come with it was immense, and I would do a "gut check," quite literally. I would assess my symptoms one at a time, not assigning "good" or "bad" to any of them but just taking stock of how I was feeling. The most important part of it for me was the checking in on my gut, because I hold so much stress there. I asked myself, is my gut in pain? If the answer was no, suddenly I noticed a relaxation there—it was my mind connecting with my body to get real in the moment. In other words, body and mind got together and determined that there wasn't a real issue—that tension I was feeling was the issue, not a real injury or physical pain—so it was okay to let it go.

- ☐ **Walk mindfully.** Feel your feet connect with the ground, notice the swing of your arms, and observe your surroundings without getting lost in thought. Walk without looking at your phone, listening to music, or any other distraction. Feel the sensations of breathing in and breathing out. Smell the grass, trees, and air. Feel the breeze on your skin.

- ☐ **Practice mindful eating.** Put your phone away. Notice the colors and textures of your food. Chew slowly and savor each bite. This is a big one in the Western world—we eat fast. It's time to sit at the table (away from the TV or streaming device), taste each morsel, and chew it thoroughly. Enjoy the act of nourishing your body.

Evening Routine

- ☐ **Detox from the digital.** Set a time to put all devices away, especially if you're looking for some clarity and inspiration to write. Sitting with a book, reading, or writing in a journal is a tactile way to get out of your head, and out of that device in your hand. Visiting museums, sightseeing, or any other activity is another opportunity to put it away. I see so many people, instead of enjoying what's in front of them, giving into the addiction of the phone. Look up, look around, and take in this beautiful world that's here to enjoy, in this one beautiful life.

☐ **Take time for reflection.** Spend a few minutes before bed reflecting on the day, acknowledging both highs and lows without judgment. This is a perfect time to journal.

MINDFULNESS SPECIFICALLY FOR WRITERS

Pre-Writing

☐ **Create a sacred space:** Designate a specific, clutter-free area for writing. Before you start, take a moment to sit quietly and simply breathe in that space. Even better, set a schedule that allows you to practice yoga first, then write after. But if that's not possible, use some of your yoga knowhow to quickly prepare for your writing session by mindfully sitting and setting up your space, then get ready to breathe.

☐ **The breath as an anchor:** Before you type or write, close your eyes and take three deep, mindful breaths. Drink in the breath; enjoy it. This signals to your brain that it's time to focus. Just as you have a ritual for arriving at the front of the mat—maybe reaching arms wide and up, then pulling them down in front of the heart with an exhale, closing the eyes, picking up the heels, and resting them back down—create your opening ritual for your writing practice.

Doing so allows you to "drop in" and get your body and mind ready to open up and create.

Mindful Writing Process

☐ **Apply mindfulness to the inner critic.** When judgmental thoughts ("This is terrible," "I can't do this") arise, simply observe them without engaging. Acknowledge the thought, then gently return your attention to the words on the page. We'll explore more about this later, but for now, remember not to fight the thought. Observe it, and move on. Writing is about forward motion. Just let your fingers fly; you can fix anything in the revision process.

☐ **Embrace writer's block.** View writer's block not as a failure, but as a sign that your mind needs to rest. Use this time for a yoga practice, a mindful walk, or a short meditation. If you're writing your own story, try writing about a different memory or exploring a new theme just to get the juices going again. And don't underestimate the power of working with someone who can objectively ask you questions and get you thinking and ready to hit the keyboard again.

- ☐ **Engage in writing as a flow state.** Instead of fixating on the final product, focus on the words as they come, one by one. Treat the act of writing as a meditation itself. This was huge for me when I wrote my first book. I didn't do it on purpose; the words fell out of me. Why? Because the story was there to tell—but I didn't know yet the order I would tell it in, the structure I would use, or even the themes of the book. Hell, it wasn't even supposed to be a book. I just typed up memories as they happened in my mind. I went back later and added details, sights, smells, and dialogue. But the first draft was just a flow—a meditation, mindfully letting the words come into my mind and flow out through my fingers. No judgement, no emotion.

Mindful Post-Writing

- ☐ **Slow down for edits.** Read your work out loud to catch typos and clunky sentences. Listen to your own voice and the rhythm of the words. This is super helpful when you're in the revision phase. When we're writing, and re-writing several times, our eyes can scan right over a confusing sentence. Reading it out loud makes the clunkiness of awkward phrasing immediately obvious.

☐ **Celebrate the small wins.** Acknowledge your progress, even if it's just a paragraph or a single page. This builds a positive feedback loop. Any writing is a win, even a small amount. It's an ongoing practice that builds over time.

06

TOOLS OF THE TRADE

Mindful Writing

Mindful writing doesn't mean crafting the perfect piece of prose; it's more about using the act of writing to build a stronger connection with yourself. But your objective isn't necessarily to sit in front of your journal or computer and think, "How will I connect with myself today?" Nor is it about worrying about content.

It's just about writing. That's it.

Whether it's premium content—the best you've ever written—or a pile of crap that you'll drag to the trash can icon later, it doesn't matter. Writing, the act of putting pen to paper or fingers to keyboard, is the accomplishment. Get in there, and get going.

Just like your yoga practice: show up.

Just as a yoga practice relies on different poses to achieve a balanced state, mindful writing uses a few key techniques to help you listen to your inner self: a compass that will point you in the direction of what you need, without you having to make a choice. Three pillars—journaling, free-writing, and stream of consciousness—each serve a unique purpose in this journey.

JOURNALING: THE PRIVATE CONVERSATION

Today, I woke up like any other day, taking a moment to stretch before sitting up and letting my feet graze the floor. Shuffling my feet as I walked to the kitchen, I yawned as I went. I fed the cats and filled the kettle for tea. Who knows why, but after washing my hands in the sink, the smell of dish soap on my hands transported me to my grandmother's house. I could see her white porcelain sink as I washed a teacup in her kitchen, the mid-morning light filtering in through floral curtains. I could almost hear her voice as she spun a tale from her place at the table, enjoying a Cuban coca and a hot cup of tea. I could smell the wood of the cabinets and feel the warmth of the time spent with her and my mother in those days. So many days. It was like a heavenly breeze had entered my heart. I smiled, ready to start the day. Ready to write.

If you already journal regularly, then you know. If you don't yet, then think of your journal as your most trusted friend and a private space where you can speak your mind without judgment. Journaling is a powerful tool for daily reflection and emotional processing. It's a way to externalize your thoughts and feelings, and get them the heck out of your head, turning them from a swirling, twirling jumble in your brain into something you can look at and work to understand. This practice is crucial for tracking personal growth over time, allowing you to see patterns in your life, acknowledge your progress, and work through challenges. It can help you refocus on your goals and get organized in your approach. And it's an ever so useful tool to keep you from taking yourself too seriously and help you, well, get over yourself.

There's an old cliché in management that goes, "Inspect what you expect." All that means is that as a manager, if you expect your employees to do something, you better be sure to inspect it, i.e., check in on their work. If you don't, your employees learn that you aren't going to check, so they aren't always motivated to complete the work that you ask for. The same thing goes for your personal growth, your goals, and your expectations. Inspect what you expect: document, make plans, vent, get it all out of you. Then, take a look at it and assess progress, revise your strategies, and try new things. It's like you're managing yourself, but in a much more pleasant way than having your boss look over your shoulder.

Before I began writing my memoir, I would journal—in spite, I admit, of my former tendency to roll my eyes anytime I heard someone talk about journaling. Honestly, there was a point when I thought maybe it was just a bit too self-indulgent. I mean, I had a diary when I was in elementary and middle school, but not beyond that. But when your thoughts and emotions, especially during turbulent times, are aching so much you just want to expel them, journaling is the place to do it. And as I progressed, I was completely won over. As I mentioned in an earlier chapter, my initial memories of my mother weren't "chapters" in a book; they were letters and journal entries, which I expanded and revised again and again to make them into something to share.

There are many ways to start journaling. **Morning pages**, a technique popularized by Julia Cameron, involves handwriting three full pages as a free-form writing exercise first thing in the morning. This practice helps clear your mind of clutter and set a focused intention for the day. For a more structured approach, you can create a **gratitude list** to shift your perspective toward what's working in your life, or use **bullet journaling** to organize your thoughts and tasks in a clear, concise way.

Guided journals can get you on the path faster than anything. They provide prompts and inspiration. Often themed, guided journals can take you toward your goals, help you figure out a health issue, establish a mindfulness practice, or find happiness in everyday life through the practice of gratitude and grace. I created a series of journals for this very purpose. I couldn't find exactly what I was looking for, so I made my own—tools that help me get the most out of my two practices, and keep me grounded in gratitude, health and happiness.

There's no wrong way to journal, and you don't need a fancy book to do it. I've always been inspired by a beautiful book in which to keep my thoughts, but there are apps you can use if you want the ease of journaling anywhere. But remember the mindful practice of unplugging: a physical book and pen that you can drop in your bag and take with you provides a little escape into your inner world without a screen, wherever you are.

FREE-WRITING: THE UNFILTERED FLOW

If journaling is a conversation, free-writing is a sprint. Its primary purpose is to bypass your inner critic. Free-writing is an exercise in getting out of your own way. The goal is simply to write, without stopping, for a set period of time.

Get rid of that head trash that stops you. If you sit in front of your computer, unsure where to start because you can't think of just the right line, the perfect beginning, plow right through that BS and just type. Type your thoughts as they come into your head. The perfect way to get going is to imagine you're talking—telling someone about something that you're interested in, a memory you have, or something you've learned. Just go for it like you would if you were in a conversation.

To practice, set a timer for five to ten minutes. When you start, your only rule is to keep the pen moving or your fingers typing. Don't worry about grammar, spelling, or if any of it makes sense. If you run out of things to say, simply write, "I don't know what to write next," until a new thought comes to you. This method trains your mind to access raw, uncensored thoughts and ideas that might otherwise remain buried.

When I started writing my memories, I didn't use a timer, so it was much more stream of consciousness; however, the method was similar. I had my sticky notes, which were my out-of-order road map, so I knew, high level, what I wanted to write about. To break through my self-judgement and doubt, I just thrust ahead and typed like I was talking to my niece or nephew, telling them a story of what it was like for me and my mom. And the flow just began; the floodgates opened.

STREAM OF CONSCIOUSNESS: THE RIVER RUNS

Stream of consciousness is the most intensive and unstructured form of mindful writing. Unlike the timed sprint of free-writing, this technique is a deep, immersive dive into the unedited flow of your mind. It's an exercise in capturing the natural, often non-linear, way in which your thoughts, memories, and emotions intertwine. It's often more poetic, fragmented, and associative than other forms of writing. Free-writing is a pre-writing exercise, while stream of consciousness is a literary technique.

When I look back on my writing, I can see how my style varies. A critic may find that unlikable in my work. But I simply don't care—changes in style, like changes in tone, are how humans think and therefore write. I'm not in it to wow someone with flair; I'm just putting stuff out there. But some of the most profound and impactful things that come through me happen when I'm in stream-of-consciousness mode. During the re-read, I often don't remember writing something and marvel that I even did that.

There's no pre-planned structure here. You simply allow your mind to be your guide. Start by focusing on a single word, feeling, or image, then allow your thoughts to unravel from there. Don't try to force a narrative. Instead, follow the threads of your thinking wherever they lead, letting memories surface and emotions bubble up without any attempt to organize them. This practice can reveal surprising connections and profound insights, offering a truly unfiltered look into your subconscious.

Beautiful prose lives within you, but when you first birth that sucker out, it may be ugly as hell. That's okay; the first objective is to get it out there. You can always go back and pretty it up later.

Put It Into Practice

Writing prompts can easily elicit a reaction, as you might read it and go, "Really?" It can sometimes be tough to see how they can help. But the idea here is to generate ideas and creativity. Get those proverbial juices flowing. That can be tough to do out of thin air, so I encourage you to have fun with these, take your time, and let your thoughts fly.

- ☐ **Cast something in the external world as a character.** Personify, or create a character out of, the external forces that create stress or fear in your life (e.g., social media, a certain boss, a difficult family member). Write a dialogue between yourself and this personified force. What do you need to say to it/ them? (Tell them what you really think!) What is it trying to tell you?

- ☐ **Give an object a voice.** Choose a random object in your home (e.g., a teacup, a bookshelf, a yoga mat). Imagine it can hold your emotions. Write from the object's perspective. What emotion did it absorb from you today? What story would it tell about your life? (Oh, the stories your mat could tell!)

- ☐ **Explore a metaphoric work of art.** Use art as inspiration to explore how you feel. If you're an artist, or want to try painting, I highly recommend it for emotional eviction. But for this exercise, if your emotion was a painting, what would it look like? If your feeling was a color and brushstroke, what would it look like and why? Write a descriptive passage about this piece of artwork. (Be descriptive with colors, whether the work is abstract or realistic, and what the subject is and why)

TIPS

☐ **See your inner critic as a protection mechanism.** Reframe the inner critic not as an enemy, but as a part of you that's trying to keep you safe from perceived failure or judgment. Give your inner critic a name. When it speaks, thank it for its input and tell it you can take it from here. (You got this!)

☐ **Try bypassing the blank page.** Start in the middle. Begin your writing session by picking a sentence from a book and continuing from there.

☐ **Use the other hand.** Using your non-dominant hand can break through creative blocks. Write a paragraph or a few sentences with your non-dominant hand. The effort required forces a different part of the brain to engage, and the slow, clumsy motion disarms the urge to be perfect.

☐ **The Three Drafts Philosophy**

  ☐ **Draft 1: The Vomit Draft.** Get everything out on the page without a filter. (My favorite part!)

  ☐ **Draft 2: The Structure Draft.** Organize and shape the ideas into a coherent narrative.

  ☐ **Draft 3: The Polish Draft.** Focus on grammar and style. This simple model gives permission to write badly first.

07

GOING DEEP
The Inner Work of Real Yoga

In Chapters 1 and 3, we spent time with the first three of Patanjali's Eight Limbs of Yoga: the Yamas, Niyamas, and Asana. The remaining five Limbs follow, progressively taking us further on the path inward. It started with the body: the physical, and the gateway to the real yoga within. Now we continue our journey inward, starting with the power of the breath.

PRANAYAMA: BREATH CONTROL

"Prana" is the vital life force energy, breath. The fourth Limb, Pranayama, involves the regulation of the breath. Through various breathing techniques, each designed for a specific purpose, the practitioner learns to control the flow of prana in the body, which has a direct impact on the state of the mind. As I'm sure you know, pranayama techniques are often included in a yoga class or meditation session. They add a beautiful layer to the process of calming the nervous system. When I was struggling, at the height of my symptoms, I would rest in a pose in Bernie's Yin Yoga classes hoping for relaxation to arrive. Bernie would start talking us through pranayama, and in some classes, my exhausted body would just pass out. On the worst days, it was the only thing that helped.

The therapeutic benefits of pranayama cannot be overstated. Not only does it help in the worst of times, as I was experiencing, but with regular incorporation into yoga classes, pranayama becomes an automatic response to a stressful situation in life. I remember the first time I noticed it, when I learned my grandmother was ill. I'd walked down the hall and sat in her chair, then noticed how deep my breath had automatically become.

Ultimately, that's the goal of the practice: when your work on the mat turns into common practice off of the mat, transforming your ability to deal with stress.

PRATYAHARA: WITHDRAWAL OF THE SENSES

The fifth Limb, Pratyahara, marks a significant turning point from the external practices to the internal journey. It is the conscious withdrawal of the senses from external distractions as you learn to be the quiet observer of your thoughts. In a world of constant sensory stimulation, this practice encourages the student to turn their awareness inward, creating a space for introspection and quieting the chatter of the mind.

But instead of actively trying to quiet that chatter, the student learns the power of observation. Either in Savasana, or just sitting still in a chair, get rid of all distractions. Take off that smart watch, and turn notifications and volume off on your phone. Observe your breath, maybe saying to yourself silently, *I am breathing in, I am breathing out.* As you lie there, or sit there comfortably, thoughts will arise. That's the nature of the mind: to create thought. *Oh look, there's a thought.* Don't try to stop the mind from thinking, but observe the thoughts as they come in. Then, instead of reacting to them, or judging the thoughts as good or bad, just let them float on by like little fluffy white clouds in the sky. *There goes that thought, right on out of here.* Bring the mind back to the breath. *I am breathing in, I am breathing out.* Again, there is stillness. Until the next thought comes in. Repeat.

DHARANA: CONCENTRATION

Building upon the inward focus of Pratyahara, the sixth Limb, Dharana, is the practice of concentration. This involves fixing the mind on a single point of focus, such as the breath, a mantra, or a visual image. For a beginner, the goal is to train the mind to remain steady and focused, reducing the tendency to be carried away by thoughts.

"Drishti" is a term you'll hear regularly in yoga classes. It's a Sanskrit word meaning "gaze" or "sight," and it's a technique used to achieve dharana. By choosing a specific focal point for your gaze—such as the tip of your nose, a thumb, or a point on the wall or floor—you give your mind an external anchor to prevent it from wandering.

This works wonders for balance. It's amazing how much of your balance is related to what's going on in your mind, not your body. Find a drishti, a gaze point, and suddenly you're more steady. Your mind is focused on that one point, not thinking about all the micro-movements of the air, or how you might fall right on your ass, taking out three of your fellow yogis practicing near you, or the table and lamp nearby if you're at home. It's a practical tool to help you train your mind for concentration, making it a key part of moving from the physical practice of yoga to the mental practice of meditation.

DHYANA: MEDITATION (CONTEMPLATION)

The seventh Limb, Dhyana, naturally arises from an unbroken state of Dharana. It's the state of meditation, where there's a continuous and effortless flow of awareness toward the object of concentration. The distinction between the practitioner and the object of focus begins to dissolve, creating a state of pure stillness and inner peace.

Dharana is the act of focusing your mind on a single point. It requires effort and willpower, like trying to keep an energetic kitten from playing. Even if you stop playing with it, that tiny cat will just keep playing on her own. You keep bringing your attention back to your breath, a mantra, or a focal point. **Dhyana** is what happens when that effort becomes effortless. It's the state of uninterrupted concentration, where you're so absorbed that you stop noticing the distractions. The mind becomes calm, and a continuous flow of awareness is established. It's like the kitten finally falls asleep in your lap (aww), and the world outside just fades away. It's the beginning of a deeper, more profound experience of consciousness.

Meditation may very well be one of the most challenging concepts in yoga—especially with our reduced attention spans. Maybe you've noticed, over the last decade or more, a growing need for instant gratification, or a reduced ability to sit and read long works for extended periods of time? Social media and our digital world of headlines, snippets, and, let's face it, snipes at each other, make it so our minds are used to receiving quick bits of information and moving on to the next thing at the speed of light.

That said, there's a way to bring the mind back to stillness, and calm all of that down. Mindfulness, absolutely—but sitting in meditation grounds that consciousness and trains the brain how to do it. I've always found the easiest way to work meditation into my day is to make it part of my yoga practice, or at least make it share the same time slot—sometimes sitting in meditation before a class, sometimes after.

Personally, I love **guided** meditation. It takes much less effort on my part, so I can just follow the cues of the teacher, and relax into the sinking sensations that ensue. But for the deepest meditation to occur, silence may be needed.

SAMADHI: UNION AND ENLIGHTENMENT

The final and eighth Limb is Samadhi, the ultimate goal of yoga. It's a state of enlightenment, of bliss, of super-consciousness where the individual self merges with universal consciousness. In this state of profound bliss and unity, the practitioner experiences a deep sense of connection to all things and a liberation from the cycle of suffering. It's the realization, and feeling in your entire being that we're all part of one big, breathing, beautiful planet—a single organism of oneness.

There is, of course, much more to explore within the deep history and concepts of yoga, but for the purpose of this book, we're sticking to a selection of ideas that will inform and inspire our writing and yoga practice. I encourage you to continue studying the deeper side of yoga. In essence, learning yoga philosophy is about moving the practice of yoga from something you do on your mat for an hour a day to the way you show up in every moment. It provides the "why" behind the "what," transforming physical exercise into a profound path of self-awareness, personal growth, and lasting inner peace. It gives a yogi the tools to not just be flexible in their body, but to be resilient, compassionate, and wise in their daily life.

So, while we're practicing yoga, are we thinking about all of that wisdom in the moment? Not really, no. That's a lot of stuff. But what your yoga teacher will likely do, is select one of the Limbs, or how to apply one of the concepts, as an inspiration or theme for a class. Many yoga practices have a theme—an area of focus that we draw our attention to, then move through the asanas with that in mind. In practicing this way, we reinforce what we've learned.

I encourage you to find your own set of intentions for your yoga practice. Each time you step on the mat, you'll likely have a little starting ritual like I do (arms up, rising onto the balls of my feet, exhaling my heels back down): an involuntary set of motions that puts you in the right headspace at the top of your mat. In that moment, set your intention for your practice. Will you be committing to being more kind to yourself? Perhaps you'll practice bearing witness to your thoughts, without judgement or opinion. Each day, your intention can vary. Revisit it at the beginning, middle, and end of your yoga class. You'll be surprised at the gifts yoga will give you when you open up to them.

The reality is that progress in mindfulness, as in asana, is not a straight line. Some days, the mind and/or body feels open and strong; other days, it feels tight and weak. The real practice is showing up with kindness and curiosity, regardless of the daily outcome, because that's when the inner growth happens. This counters the perfectionist, goal-oriented mindset so prevalent in our culture. And if we're open to receive, progress and creativity will naturally flow. Ideas and moments of pure clarity will pop right into your head. Then, with gratitude, you can give right back to your loved ones, your community, and your planet.

THE ORIGINAL TRUTH

Beyond the poses, the deeper work of yoga is not a destination to be reached; it is developing a skill for listening to the wisdom we are born with. Here, we shed the stories the world and society have given us so that we can finally reach our truest selves. The ancient principles teach us excavation of the soul, brushing away the dust of the years to find our most solid foundation--our truth.

THE SOMATIC INQUIRY:

Find a comfortable seat on a cushion. Sit toward the front edge of it to let your pelvis tilt slightly forward, allowing your spine to reach tall up through the crown of your head. Place both hands on the upper part of your belly. Close your eyes and take a deep breath in through your nose, and let it out slowly through the mouth. What original parts of your truth would you like to bring back? What advice would your nine-year-old self give to you today?

Put It Into Practice

This is a little homework assignment that will help you integrate these principles into your yoga and writing practice. When I began my commitment to yoga, I read many texts on the foundations of the practice and philosophy, but they never really stuck until I made myself an example to-do list—a way of taking the concepts and turning them into reality.

Now it's your turn. Get out a journal or a notebook and a pen. Flip back to chapter 1, starting with the Yamas. Go through each foundational concept, jot down a quick definition (a few words), and come up with one way in which you can integrate it into your practice. Continue by coming back to this chapter and working through the rest of the Eight Limbs.

List each guiding principle, define it in your own words, and make a note about how you'll use it in your life, your yoga, or your writing.

Before you look at my example, go ahead and give it a try yourself. This is an awesome exercise that will not only help you remember the purpose and goal of each of the Limbs and their components, but also give you an action plan for integrating them into your yoga and/or writing practice.

Guiding Principle	Meaning	How I'll Use It
Ahimsa	Don't be a jerk	When I notice negative self-talk about how flexible I am (or not), I will instead be kind and accepting.
Satya	Honesty	I'll always tell the truth, but when I see Susan's new haircut, I may keep my thoughts to myself.
Brahmacharya	Don't waste energy	I'll put down my phone and stop my tendency to scroll and work on my next book instead.
Aparigraha	Don't be greedy	I'll do what I love, what lights me up and brings joy, and not worry about what things I have or think I need to get.
Saucha	Clean living	I'll make my yoga space clear of clutter, and nourish my body with the most nutrient dense foods.
Santosha	Be content	I'll always remember to look for that little place inside that's always happy, for no particular reason at all.

Guiding Principle	Meaning	How I'll Use It
Tapas	Bring it!	I'll challenge myself to grow in my asana practice, turning on the fire when needed to build strength.
Svadhyaya	The comedy of me	I'll stay open to self-study and learning about me—and accept whatever I find.
Ishvara Pranidhana	Letting go	At the end of my yoga practice, and when I sit down in front of my laptop to write, I'll remember to give up control—and be a human being, not always a human doing, letting creativity flow through me.
Asana	The poses	I'll practice yoga just about every day, not judging how my poses look, but feeling my way into them.
Pranayama	The breath	Every day, I'll find time to focus on my breath, even if just for a minute, using my calming superpower so that it becomes automatic.

Guiding Principle	Meaning	How I'll Use It
Pratyahara	The observer	As I lie in Savasana, or sit in meditation, I'll allow thoughts to arrive, and I'll watch them float on by—no judgement.
Dharana	Focus	When balancing in yoga, I'll focus on a drishti, a gaze point, to help me balance.
Dhyana	Meditation	I'll integrate meditation into my practice daily, so that the effortless concentration of dharana happens naturally.
Samadhi	Peace	I will not seek samadhi as a goal; rather, I'll understand that it's all a journey.

08

ART IS LIFE
Writing is Art, Writing is Life

Amazing things can happen in the midst of illness and trauma. It's unlikely that they'll seem amazing at the time; they'll just seem like survival. But I experienced something as I was coming out of the worst of it that really didn't strike me as meaningful until I wrote about it. The following passage was originally written as advice to my lovely niece. I thought about including it in my memoir but decided against it. I suppose I could have left it in, but I didn't feel like it served my themes. I'm including it here because it's a powerful way of looking at art—and while I was talking about painting, it applies absolutely to writing. It's a little piece about the healing power of expression and getting what's inside, out.

ART IS LIFE

The secret to creating real art is not giving a damn about what anyone else thinks. Easier said than done, of course, but that ability is a gift that's freeing. Because art is art, and it doesn't have to be "good." Because what is good, anyway? "Good" is wholly subjective to the speaker of the word. There is no "good" in art; there is only expression. And if it's your expression, it's yours to express, so there's no wrong answer. And once you get that, you understand those pieces you've seen in museums and thought, "Well, that's not great; I could do that." Maybe you could, but you didn't. That artist had something to say, and they said it with paint, or lead, or sculpted iron. Does it have to be pretty? No. Does it have to be lifelike? No. It just has to *be*. That is art.

If there is expression, then there is art.

When I started my private tour through hell, otherwise known as coming down with a seemingly unknowable ailment, I started to paint—and paint big. When Mom first got sick six years earlier, I baked cakes like a crazy person—as an outlet for stress. That was the beginning of my habit of taking up a new hobby when under duress. This time, it was painting. I'd never done any painting before, but I went down to the art store and, with my husband Ricky's help, procured a stack of small practice boards and a few giant canvases, about 4 feet tall and 5 feet wide. Why so huge? I just felt like I had something to say, and it felt big. I bought brushes of all sizes and acrylic paint in many colors. I began with the practice boards, trying my hand at painting cherry blossoms on branches, and a silhouette of a human figure in front of a sunset. They were what I'd call "restrained." And then Ricky gave me a fantastic tip.

"Put on some headphones, play some good music, and then just paint—see what happens."

That's when the big canvases came out, and the big tubes of paint. I placed old sheets on the floor as drop cloths. I used an old plastic container as a pallet. And I just let it happen. I had a vague idea of images I wanted to paint, but I didn't work from life or from photos. I knew I wanted to paint cherry blossoms, bamboo, rain, and the sea. The first was what could be best described as a black and white bamboo forest in the rain. I carefully worked on the bamboo stalks, one at a time. I tried to make them as recognizable as possible, which wasn't too hard, but some of them looked weird, and I was unhappy with the result. I dunked my brush in water and started swiping at the stalks I didn't like. They started to blend, the different tones of paint mixing together, and creating this rainy, washed-out look. I kept going, swiping and blending, adding more paint, swiping some more, up and down. Next to the few stalks I left, I had what I wanted, and it looked like I felt. A few perfect stalks surrounded by sad and angry brushstrokes in tones of gray, black, and white. It felt like I'd let something out of myself.

Next was the moon over the ocean at night, its reflection sparkling on the water, and stars in the sky. This time, I worked from a photo, but the sea looked more rough than in the image that inspired the painting. The moon was bigger, the sky darker. It looked like I felt—haunted, reflective—but the image was strangely calming. I put a star in the sky for every year Ricky and I had been together: eight, at that time.

Then, the ocean. Just water and sky, this time. I blended greens and blues to get water that looked like the unique colors down in the Keys. Almost white in places, and deeply indigo in others, it looked like the night sea blending into the day. This one was more serene, and it made me feel so. More canvases, and more ocean. I painted like I felt—urgent, without control, full. And I painted what I longed for: peace.

Would anyone think they were "good?" I don't care, and it doesn't matter. It was therapeutic as hell.

I still paint from time to time, but the giant canvases are gone. I work small, painting beautiful scenes in nature—places I want to go. My work is more controlled. I work from photos. I'm patient, taking weeks to complete a work, when those huge canvases were completed in an afternoon.

We judge our lives, as we judge art, as "good" or not. But the truth is just as there is only expression in art, there is only living a life. Does it have to be pretty? No. Do we? No. Does it have to be like everyone else's? No. Does it have to be a straight path? No. Isn't it better when it's none of those things? It just has to *be*, and that's good enough. We have something to say, and we say it through our decisions, our love, our contributions, our art, our generosity, and our actions. We feel what we feel, we are who we are, we bloom how we bloom, and we will become who we will become.

There is only one right way to do that, and it is ours alone. Pop in a playlist, and see what happens.

Writing is art. Your canvas is the page, your paintbrush the pen. Your story is completely and utterly unique, because it will happen in your voice if you find a way to put your voice on the page. Let us hear, see, and feel what you have to say.

Mindful writing, like a yoga practice, is not about the final product but about the journey of showing up. Bring yourself fully into it, give us the gift of your words, for it is you that makes your writing amazing—not the events that transpired, but how you tell them and what you do with your experiences. How did they change you, what did you learn, and what can you offer to others? It's not even about the words themselves, but what comes through the words.

Embrace the mess, the imperfection, and the process as a sacred part of self-discovery. There is wisdom to be found within you; you just have to dive in to get it.

09

BREATH
The Yogi's Superpower

Here's that yogi superpower I mentioned: the skill to chill. Seriously, your breath is the most underrated therapeutic tool you have. Let's explore how conscious breathing can calm your nervous system faster than watching *Friends* and how different breathing techniques can either energize you for a big day or lull you into a state of blissful calm.

At the peak of my symptoms, I wasn't sleeping—like, hardly at all. It was a miserable existence of praying for sleep all night, and just not getting sleepy. I was exhausted, but I couldn't get sleepy. My poor body, malnourished because my stomach would barely accept food, was broken. I had no idea what to do—the doctors had given up on me by this time, and I was at a total loss. I turned to yoga. I found Yin Yoga, the slowest of the slow yoga, and gave it a shot.

The first thing Bernie had us do was sit cross-legged and "arrive." He said to just arrive on the mat, be here, now. Nothing else mattered, just this moment. Then we started to breathe deeply, just a few breaths at the beginning of the class, before we moved into our first long-held Yin pose. We breathed in for a four count: in, two, three, four, slowly. Then we let that breath out for a six count: out, two, three, four, five, six, even slower. One breath in, and something shifted inside of me. I felt a sense of calm, ever so delicate, whisper through my entire being. I could tell right away that peace was still within me, but I needed some tools to go in and get it. I knew I had come to the right place, and I couldn't wait to find out what yoga could do.

As we moved into the first pose, Bernie talked me through getting into the right position, and adjusting it to meet my needs. Then we became still, and just let that pose marinate, opening the connective tissues of the body. While we held the pose, Bernie talked. I learned about the parasympathetic and sympathetic nervous systems.

The body's autonomic nervous system, which controls involuntary bodily functions like heart rate, breathing, and digestion, operates through a constant and delicate balance between two opposing forces: the sympathetic and the parasympathetic nervous systems. The sympathetic nervous system is your body's fight-or-flight response. When a threat or stressor presents itself, whether it's a real danger or a big meeting at work, it kicks in. Hormones like adrenaline and cortisol are released, and that increases your heart rate and raises your blood pressure. Blood flow is diverted to your muscles in preparation for quick action. It's an essential survival mechanism, but when it's constantly activated due to chronic stress, it can lead to anxiety, fatigue, and other health issues.

Well, I knew right away that my sympathetic nervous system was in overdrive, because what he described was my life. I was in a constant state of fight-or-flight, and it wasn't just due to chronic stress. My body was severely overreacting to everyday life as well as to stress, and I described it at the time as feeling like I'd been poisoned. Then Bernie got down to the nitty gritty of what this way of breathing could do.

The parasympathetic nervous system is the "rest-and-digest" system. It acts as the body's brake pedal, promoting a state of calm and restoration. When activated, it lowers your heart rate, decreases blood pressure, and directs energy toward vital functions like digestion and tissue repair. This system is crucial for a healthy balance, allowing the body to recover and heal from the demands of daily life. For most people, the sympathetic nervous system fires a bit too much, making it difficult to fully relax and recuperate; for me, it was on 24/7. I desperately needed my rest-and-digest system to kick in.

I learned that this is where the breath becomes a powerful tool. By consciously controlling your breathing, you can directly influence your nervous system. Fast, shallow breaths—how we naturally breathe when stressed—reinforce the sympathetic response. In contrast, slow, deep, and deliberate breathing, particularly with an emphasis on a longer exhale, sends a signal to your brain via the vagus nerve that you're safe. All is well, and it's okay to let the muscles relax and send you into a rest state, or even sleep. The signal activates the parasympathetic nervous system, effectively telling your body to stand down from its fight-or-flight mode.

As Bernie talked, and had us practice slow, deep inhales followed by long exhales, my battered and broken body, which just would not sleep at night, started to melt. And it was there, on my mat, where I would nod off. Finally, something was bringing my body back to rest. I started practicing every day, sometimes twice a day, just to feel that relief. Even though it wasn't taking me into long naps, just the feeling of relaxation deep enough to let me slip into sleep for a minute or two was an absolute gift. I would do Bernie's classes that were an hour to an hour and a half long—the longer the better, just to feel that wonderful letting go.

This physiological effect, the activating of the parasympathetic nervous system, is at the core of a practice like Yin Yoga. The stillness and the prolonged stretches into connective tissues are paired with a focus on deep, slow abdominal breathing. As you remain in a pose and direct your breath to areas of sensation, you are consciously overriding the sympathetic impulse to tense up or flee the discomfort. The combination of prolonged stillness and deep breathing coaxes the nervous system to shift from a state of vigilance to one of deep relaxation, allowing the parasympathetic nervous system to take over and restore a sense of calm and equilibrium.

This miracle of breath can be achieved just as easily when sitting in your chair, as it can in a Yin Yoga pose on the mat. Once you know what you're doing, you can do it walking down the street or in a meeting. Practicing pranayama regularly in your yoga practice—and you should always learn how at the instruction of a trained teacher—will eventually lead to automatic calming through breath, in your daily life.

Pranayama encompasses a wide range of breathing techniques, each designed to produce a specific effect on the body and mind by controlling the flow of prana, or life force energy. While deep diaphragmatic breathing in a passive pose (like in Yin Yoga) is a foundational practice, many other forms of pranayama are used to either calm, energize, or balance the system.

NADI SHODHANA (ALTERNATE NOSTRIL BREATHING)

This is a gentle, balancing practice that involves inhaling through one nostril and exhaling through the other in a rhythmic pattern. Generally, the first two fingers of one hand are placed on the third eye (the forehead between the eyes). The thumb is placed on one nostril, and the ring finger on the other. Plug one nostril and inhale slowly through the open one, plug both nostrils to hold the breath for a beat, then unplug the opposite nostril and exhale more slowly still. Your teacher will have you repeat this for the duration of the Nadi Shodhana session. This exercise is said to purify the nadis, or energy channels, and balance the two hemispheres of the brain. The left nostril is associated with the ida nadi and lunar (cooling, calming) energy, while the right nostril is linked to the pingala nadi and solar (heating, activating) energy. By alternately breathing through each side, you harmonize these energies.

Nadi Shodhana is known for its ability to reduce stress, calm the nervous system, improve focus, and prepare the mind for meditation. It's an excellent technique for managing anxiety and slowing everything down, allowing more of a sense of inner peace.

KAPALABHATI (BREATH OF FIRE)

This is an invigorating and cleansing practice. It involves a series of forceful, short exhalations powered by the abdominal muscles, with the inhalation happening passively and automatically. The rapid, pumping motion of the diaphragm is said to create heat in the body and cleanse the respiratory system. Definitely only practice Kapalabhati at the direction of a trained teacher, as dizziness or light-headedness has been known to occur in some students.

Kapalabhati energizes the body and mind, increases circulation, and is believed to detoxify the system. Because of its stimulating nature, it's often used to improve mental clarity. It's generally not recommended for people with high blood pressure or heart conditions.

UJJAYI (OCEANIC BREATH)

This is a common breath used in the more active yoga styles, like Vinyasa and Ashtanga. It involves slightly constricting the back of the throat on both the inhale and the exhale, creating a soft, audible sound that resembles the ocean's waves. Hold your hand up, palm toward your mouth, and act like you're fogging a mirror, making a soft "haaaa" sound as you exhale. That's the sound—now do that with your mouth closed, and continue to constrict the back of the throat in the same way to make the sound on both inhales and exhales. This constriction helps to regulate the flow of air, allowing for a longer, more controlled breath.

Ujjayi creates internal heat and helps to build a sense of rhythm and focus in a physical yoga practice. The sound of the breath itself acts as a meditative anchor, helping to quiet the mind and link movement to breath. It also helps to calm the nervous system and can be used to soothe and ground during stressful moments. In a live class and during some of the more challenging poses, a room full of yogis will start sounding like a weird chorus of giant crickets as they all work through the flow together, Ujjayi breathing, one and all.

Pranayama is basically the most advanced tool you have for managing your own energy, and it's something you carry with you all the time. It's as if your nervous system is a car. The sympathetic nervous system is the gas pedal, and the parasympathetic nervous system is the brake. Pranayama is the driver. With a few conscious breaths, you can hit the gas to get energized, hit the brake to calm down, or find that sweet spot in between for perfect cruise control.

With a daily practice that was giving me what no medication, doctor, or anything else could accomplish, it's no wonder I was hooked. I knew the power of the practice now, and it started to provide clarity in other ways. I was learning how to pay close attention to my body, and now I was really listening.

PRESENCE: FINDING THE HERE AND NOW

In this crazy life full of notifications and endless scrolling, presence is practically an act of defiance. It's a stand that we must take; deciding to take better care of ourselves. This was an unexpected gift of yoga for me, and it's one for which I'll forever be grateful. Yoga teaches mindfulness easily, and you learn, just by showing up on the mat, to notice little things in the here and now. That does wonders for your nervous system, as they say that anxiety is worry for the future, depression is worry for the past, and relaxation is here in the present. But the ability to be consciously present—well, that's like being awake when the rest of the world is walking around asleep.

There's no better way to bring yourself into the here and now than by focusing on the breath. Tuning into the body is all presence, for the body only knows *now*. Noticing the breath, and bringing the mind back to it again and again: that's when the rest of the world falls away, and we become calm. It's proof that in the present moment, there's nothing to fear, nothing to worry about.

Yoga and diet were the two tools that rescued me from the depths of my undiagnosed chronic illness. And as I was slowly getting to my new normal, I leaned into everything that brought me joy: my husband, my family, my favorite places, my yoga. My mother and I spent many long weekends traveling to Key West to visit my grandmother. Her house was a safe place for me, a cocoon of love and energy that filled me up. The three of us were something else, and all together, we were three parts of a whole. And it was there, at my grandmother's kitchen table, over Cuban cocas (rolls) and hot tea, that I realized I needed to really pay attention. I listened intently to every story she told, even if I'd heard it before. I tuned into the sound of her voice, the way she kicked her feet up like a teenager, and how she buttered her bread. I knew that we wouldn't always have that time, and I really noticed and decided to remember it all.

And oh, dear friend, am I glad I did. Two years after the peak of my symptoms, my dearest Gramma left this world. If I hadn't gotten sick, and therefore found my yoga and mindfulness practice, I fear I may have glided through those years, not visiting her as much and not listening, watching, and taking in every precious moment. I gathered all of it purposefully and carefully, and now all those memories live on with me.

I lost my mom just twenty months after Gramma. I had four years of mindful memory making—and that directly fueled my memoir writing later. While we may begin our yoga practice for physical exercise, or because we feel stressed, the skills we learn pay off way beyond the mat. Pay attention, be present, and someday you'll realize what you captured: something precious and special that you can keep with you, always.

BENEFITS: FINDING YOGA

I studied; I practiced. For a while, it was survival: my hours on the mat were the only time I felt any kind of good, and the rest of life was a struggle. But my yoga taught me some things that got me through, lessons to carry always:

∞ **Keep going.** On days when I'm weary and not wanting to do much, that's okay—I select a yoga practice that meets me where I am that day. I match the class to the effort I'm able to bring. I listen to my body and practice in a way that's kind and gentle when I need it to be. Out in life, with my writing, at work, with obligations, I applied the same philosophy— and I never let my illness stop me. I didn't run myself into the ground, either. I accelerated when I could, and I took my foot off the gas when I needed it. But I kept going—and that showed me strength from within that I never knew I possessed.

∞ **Breath is power.** With practice, it worked its way into my daily life, and I found I had a new way of dealing with stress. And the best part was learning that I had access to deep peace, any time I needed it. Because yoga is "remembering," I now knew that I didn't have to search for peace and joy. I AM immense peace. I AM stillness. I AM joy. I only need to go inside myself, where it lives always, to find it.

∞ **I wasn't alone.** This community of beautiful souls, of seekers, of light workers and healers, took me in. The yoga community is welcoming, and if you find your team, your tribe, one that's not caught up in the visual weirdness of social media (they may use it, but not in purely superficial ways), it's a priceless experience. So many here are just in it to help each other, and to help as many people as we can find. And if you came to yoga with trauma, or chronic illness, or grief—so did so many others. Each yoga story is a unique ride, but some of us arrived on the same train.

ALL IS ONE

Our breath is a delicate, invisible river that flows between the past to the future. It is the only thing we share with every ancestor who ever lived, and every descendant yet to come. In the Middle of Always, your inhale is an invitation to receive your unique history, and each exhale is an opportunity to let it go.

THE SOMATIC INQUIRY:
Close your eyes. As you sit there breathing, notice each inhale and each exhale. Don't try to breathe a certain way, or manipulate the breath to be what you think it should be in this moment. Simply observe, "I am breathing in. I am breathing out." Joyously celebrate your breath. Ask: what is one gift that your breath has given you?

Put It Into Practice

Write a journal entry that explores how you will commit to finding presence. Make it a series of commitments:

- ☐ List the ways in which you will purposefully mine for presence in your interactions with others, especially those you are close to or want to be closer to.

- ☐ Outline how you'll practice more presence in your yoga practice: as you step to the mat, during the poses themselves, and after practice.

- ☐ How will you create a habit of finding presence in your writing practice, and what does that mean to you?

10

BRINGING IT TO LIFE
The Essentials of Story

In a Chapter 15, we'll get into the phases of writing your story or memoir with a roadmap that will help you take a pile of memories and make an engaging story out of them, whether for yourself, your family, or the world at large. First, just as we've covered the basics of yogic philosophy, here we'll review some of the basics of writing story. Admittedly, reading about writing essentials can sometimes have the effect of intimidating the will to write right out of you. So, while these concepts and techniques will help you in the writing process, think of them as items that you may use now, or not, but you'll be sure to work through and include as you go through the revision process later. Maybe keep them in mind as you begin to write, but don't let the pressure of trying to get all of this "right" stifle your creativity.

Writing is a flow, and you have to let that river run, my friend. So, give these essentials a read now, and keep them in the back of your mind as you go. Then come back when you're ready to get into the revision process, refining and structuring your story.

Take a moment to acknowledge where you are. You're reading this, so I can only assume that you're committed to writing in some form, and integrating it with your yoga practice. That decision you made, that commitment, to pay attention to and tell your story, is a bold and brave move. You're taking ownership of your history and setting sail on a journey of the self. Celebrate this moment. Acknowledge the importance of it, the lessons of your past that you'll reveal or uncover, as you give the gift of your words, your story in the wash.

Embarking on a journey of self-exploration through writing is a powerful and revealing act. While the content of your story is unique to you, there are a number of techniques that can help you translate your experiences onto the page with greater depth and impact by sharing universal truth. This chapter will provide an overview of these essential tools, providing you with a deeper understanding of how to craft a compelling and honest narrative of your life. For it is in the refinement of your story that the pure exploration and perspective shifts can happen. That can occur in the first draft, sure, but as you go back and weave in these essentials to further refine your story, you'll be like a sculptor revealing the work of art that was there all along—the truest you.

POINT OF VIEW AND VOICE

Choosing your **point of view** is the first major decision you make when writing a memoir. The most common and impactful perspective is the **first person** ("I"), as it immediately establishes an intimate and personal connection with the reader—as if you're speaking directly to them and taking them along on your adventures. By using "I," you invite the reader directly into your thoughts, feelings, and experiences, allowing them to see the world through your eyes. That said, a helpful technique for writing about your own life can be to write about it in the third person. That exercise may help you get more of the details out, as it detaches you from the experience and you become more of the casual observer we talked about. But if you intend to share the story with others, you'll likely want to change it back to first person to keep it engaging.

Closely related to point of view is your **voice**, which is your personality as it comes through in your writing. It's probably the one thing that matters most in memoir and communicating your story. The events that happened to you may be unique, or they may not be; it's what you do with them, what you have to say about them, and how you say it that are the real reasons someone will want to read your story. It's the unique way in which you express yourself, a blend of your word choices, sentence structure, and overall style. Your voice is what makes your writing sound like *you*. For example, one writer might have a funny, conversational voice, while another's might be more formal and reflective. Both can resonate with certain readers, but the most important thing is that the voice is yours. Keep it real.

Tone, on the other hand, is the attitude you take toward your subject matter. If you're writing about a difficult memory, your tone might be somber or empathetic, even if your overall voice is generally the same as it was throughout the rest of your writing. Just as it would if you were speaking, your tone may change based on the conversation, but it's still you talking. I get most immersed in a memoir if it feels like I'm in a conversation with the author, as if they're telling me the story of their life. Reading your writing out loud can help you determine if your inner voice has come through. Understanding the difference between voice and tone will help you maintain consistency and create a narrative that will resonate with the reader. While tone may change based on the subject matter, voice can and should remain yours.

THEME, PLOT, AND CONFLICT

In memoir, the **plot** is the sequence of events that happened in your life, plain and simple. But what gives those events meaning is the **theme**: the central idea, message, or question that your story explores. In a memoir, the theme often drives the plot. For instance, the plot might be the story of you starting a new business, while the underlying theme is the journey of finding courage or learning to trust yourself. Identifying the theme of your story early on can help you decide which events to include and how to shape them. I had drafted my complete memoir manuscript by the time I started really thinking about themes. My process was a therapeutic one, and I had powered through the initial letters and draft in an effort to get through a tough time. But when I started thinking about themes, it was in an effort to make sure that my chapters, events, and conclusions all supported those themes, instead of being a random stack of memories. I realized that my story had a few themes, the big ones being my quest for health and becoming a self-advocate, the role reversal that happens when a child becomes the caretaker, and the profound power of writing to change perspective. All that had come out in the story naturally, but now I had to go back and get rid of, or change, some content to ensure the pieces of my story were supporting my themes and moving the narrative forward.

Every story, even one about your own life, needs **conflict**. Conflict creates tension and propels the narrative forward. This likely won't be too hard to come up with, as conflict in our lives is usually the impetus for wanting to write our story in the first place: *I went through some pretty serious crap; I should write a book.* In memoir, this conflict often comes from different sources: **person vs. person** (a disagreement with a family member, coworker, or other relationship), **person vs. society** (navigating a social norm you disagree with), **person vs. nature** (facing a challenge in the wilderness, an illness, or the limitations of your own body), or, most importantly for self-exploration, **person vs. self** (the internal struggle with your own doubts, fears, and beliefs). And, of course, more than one may apply. By honestly exploring these conflicts, you reveal the inner turmoil and growth that define your story. For me, it was person, nature, and self beating each other up all over the place.

YOUR STORY ARC

The story arc of your memoir is the journey of your transformation. It's the change in your perspective, the shift in your understanding, the psychological or emotional journey you undertook. It's the real reason readers will pick up your book. Every effective memoir has one. Where did you begin, what happened, and how did that change you? For it's the transformation that's attractive to readers. They don't just want to know what happened to you; they want to know what it did for you, what you learned, and how they too might learn from your experience.

The arc of a story has four parts: the **stasis** (your life before the story began), the **inciting incident** (the event that sets your story in motion), the **rising action** (the series of moments where you grapple with your new reality), and the **climax/resolution** (the moment of greatest tension or realization, i.e., the turning point of the story and the new understanding you've gained and new life you've built as a result). What did you learn through your experiences? The story arc is the map of that learning.

So, how do you choose what kind of arc to use for your story? Unlike a novel, your memoir doesn't have a pre-written plot. You have to find the story within the events at your disposal and your memories. The structure you choose will be the skeleton that holds your narrative together. There are a few common approaches.

The **chronological arc** is the most straightforward. You tell your story from point A to point B, following the timeline of events. This works best when your story has a clear, linear progression with a defined beginning, middle, and end. Think of a journey from childhood to adulthood, or a period of recovery from an illness.

Using a **thematic arc**, you organize your story around a central idea or theme rather than a strict timeline. For example, a memoir about finding your voice might jump between different periods of your life, all united by that central theme. This is a powerful choice for exploring a single, complex idea.

A **braided arc** is a more advanced technique that weaves together two or more timelines or thematic threads. You might alternate chapters between your childhood and your present-day life, showing how the past has influenced the person you are today. This creates suspense and rich layers of meaning but requires careful planning to ensure the timelines connect gracefully.

What feels like the most natural way to tell your story? Is there a clear beginning and end? Or are there multiple threads and ideas that could be woven together? Choose one structure and write a simple outline.

ADDING DEPTH: SUBTEXT, IMAGERY, AND SYMBOLISM

Subtext is the unspoken part of your story: the thoughts, emotions, and intentions that lie beneath the surface of what's being said or done. It's what makes a scene feel layered and real. You can create subtext by describing a character's body language, showing their actions rather than just telling the reader what they're feeling, or hinting at something important without explicitly stating it. For example, a character might say, "I'm fine," while wrapping their arms around their middle and casting their eyes downward, revealing an inner pain or anxiety.

To bring your memories to life for the reader, you can use **imagery**—language that appeals to the five senses. Instead of saying, "the walkway around the nature center was sunny," describe the warmth of the sun on a character's skin, the smell of the dampness in the wooden boardwalk, and the soft breeze that lifts your hair. This **show, don't tell** technique is super important. It's what really starts to turn your journal entries into prose for someone else to read and feel and understand. For instance, instead of saying, "I was so sad," you could write, "A heavy feeling settled in my chest, the same burden and stifling weight I'd carried for months." This more descriptive approach allows the reader to experience your emotions with you. I didn't bother too much with this in the first draft, but I went back and revised everything using this approach. And it wasn't always easy. Turning your memories into a scene requires you to really go back there in your mind and feel that experience and everything that went with it. I'm not saying you should do it the same way I did, but for me, my initial creative process wasn't slowed by me trying to be descriptive and bringing the reader with me—that came later.

You can further enrich your writing with **figurative language** like **similes** (using "like" or "as" to compare two things) and **metaphors** (stating that one thing *is* another). A simile might be "his laugh was like a broken moorhen," while a metaphor could be "my grief was a silent, gray cloud that followed me everywhere." Additionally, **symbolism** allows objects, people, or events to stand for a deeper idea. A house in the swamp might symbolize a retreat away from the world, or a specific song might symbolize tapping into power and freedom learned while running as a child.

FLASHBACK, FORESHADOWING, AND SETTING

Your story may not always be a linear progression of events. **Flashbacks** are moments in the narrative where you jump back in time to reveal important backstory that sheds light on the present. They can provide crucial context for a character's motivations or offer clarity around what led to a current event. They can also help with the flow of the story. For example, if you want to introduce the central conflict in the first chapter—which is a good idea, since you want to grab the reader with the most interesting part of the story, then unfold how you got there—you may have to set the first chapter in the present day or at least later in the timeline, then in subsequent chapters go back in time to tell the story chronologically. But be careful with bouncing around in time too much, as it can get confusing for the reader. **Foreshadowing**, on the other hand, is the use of hints or clues about what will happen later in the story. This technique can create suspense and give your narrative a sense of inevitability: "We didn't know then that her leaving that way would echo through time, and one day I would have to make an escape of my own."

The **setting** of your story is more than just a backdrop. It can be a character in itself, influencing the **atmosphere** and mood of the narrative. The cramped, chaotic kitchen of your childhood home might reflect the family's disfunction, or a serene mountaintop might become a symbol of personal peace. Describe the setting with rich, sensory detail to make it a living, breathing part of your story. The city and island of Key West is practically a character in my story, because it was so much a part of our lives that I had to give the reader a sense of what it was like to be there. Hopefully, I accomplished that.

CHARACTER, DIALOGUE, AND REVISION

In memoir, the central character is **you**. Writing for self-exploration requires an honest and unflinching look at yourself, including your flaws, contradictions, and moments of growth. In so doing, remember to connect with the universal nature of those characteristics, as you are part of that oneness I mentioned. We're all different, but not *so* different. You are also a dynamic and evolving person, not a static figure. Showing this evolution is what makes a memoir interesting. The arc of the story should be your evolution.

When you include **dialogue**, it should sound authentic to the person speaking. Use **dialogue tags** like "he said" or "she asked" sparingly, and when you can, replace them with **action beats**—small actions that reveal the speaker's emotions. For example, instead of writing "'I guess so,' she said sadly," you could write, "She shrugged and looked away. 'I guess so.'"

Revision is a crucial part of the process. This is where you begin shaping your story. I like to think of the revision process as sculpting. Over many weeks, months, or even years, you chip away at it. Shaping, trimming, adding, and molding the story and narrative into what you want takes time, patience, and perseverance.

Start with **big-picture revisions**, focusing on the overall structure and flow. Do you need to move a scene? Is the theme clear? Then move to **line-by-line edits**, polishing your sentences and correcting grammar. Also, seeking feedback from trusted readers can provide new perspectives and help you see your work with fresh eyes. When you're getting to the final stages of revision, you may want to go to an online platform like Reedsy and hire a freelance editor. There, you can see their portfolio of work, and find someone who has expertise in memoir specifically. If you choose to invest in that service, it adds a layer of polish to your work.

Writing a memoir is a deeply personal exercise, and it can be draining. After I dumped mine out of me in the span of a couple of months, I stepped away. I was exhausted, needing to heal physically and emotionally from the experience of trying to get diagnosed while writing it. Months later, when I felt ready, I started to come back to it. I would read a little here, a little there, shocked by the fact that I'd accomplished the writing itself. And I began the revision process, which took a very long time for me. Facing all of the trauma and grief, I went through the manuscript again and again over time—refining, making small changes and sometimes big ones. Eventually, it's like I'd sculpted it into something I was willing to share with the world. And it was in the revision process, not the initial drafting, that my biggest revelations happened. That's when, as I read with more of an outside eye, I was able to see more clearly and find grace and forgiveness for the main character—me.

OVERCOMING CHALLENGES AND ETHICAL CONSIDERATIONS

Every writer experiences **writer's block** at some point. The key is to keep moving forward. Try freewriting without judgment, changing your writing location, or setting a timer for small bursts of writing. For me, most often it would happen with a difficult memory, and my mind would just shut me down—and I'd feel tired and deflated. So, I changed the subject. I would bounce to a happier memory and just write about that. I kept coming back to the others and, over time, got it done. There are a bunch of prompts in this book to help you out. The most important thing is to simply begin again.

Writing a memoir also comes with **ethical considerations**. Since you're writing about real people and events, you must be mindful of their privacy and your own perspective. Remember that your story is your truth, but it's only one truth. It's essential to consider how your narrative might impact others and, where necessary, to change names or identifying details to protect their privacy.

PUT IT INTO PRACTICE

This exercise will help you begin to identify and articulate the foundational elements of your story, even if you're not ready to commit to a full outline yet. The goal is to get some initial ideas flowing and see what naturally emerges from your river of thoughts. Remember, there's no right or wrong answer here—it's just pure exploration.

The inciting incident. Think about the story you want to tell. What was the absolute beginning of the "story" part of your life? This isn't necessarily your birth, but the event or moment that truly set the narrative in motion. It's the spark that lit the flame.

- ☐ In your journal or a new document, freewrite for five to seven minutes about this inciting incident.

- ☐ Don't worry about perfect prose. Just describe what happened, how it felt, and what shifted in your life as a result.

- ☐ Who was involved? Where did it happen? What was the immediate aftermath?

The core conflict. Every story has a central conflict—an internal or external struggle that drives the narrative forward. This isn't just a problem, but the main challenge your "character" (you!) faced.

- [ ] After a short break, free-write for another five to seven minutes.

- [ ] What was the biggest struggle or challenge you faced during the period of your life you're writing about? Was it a battle with yourself, a difficult relationship, an external circumstance, or all of the above?

- [ ] Describe this conflict in your own words. How did it manifest in your daily life? What was at stake for you?

The transformation. Even if your story isn't fully written, you likely have an idea of how this conflict, or the journey itself, changed you. It doesn't have to be a big transformation; it may be a small one. What was the shift, however subtle, from the beginning to a later point in your story?

- [ ] For the final five to seven minutes, free-write about any small or large transformation you experienced as a result of confronting your conflict or moving through the events of your story.

□ How are you different from who you were at the beginning? What did you learn? What new insights or perspectives did you gain?

Reflection (optional, but recommended). After completing the three free-writing sessions, take a moment to read what you've written. Don't judge it, just observe.

□ What connections do you notice between the inciting incident, the conflict, and your transformation?

□ Are there any surprising insights or strong emotions that emerged?

This is how you start to tap into the raw material of your story. You don't need to revise it now. Simply acknowledge what you've unearthed. Keep these insights in mind as you continue your writing practice.

11

IN THE FLOW
An Invitation to Explore

When you learn something life-changing, it's natural to want to share it with the world. In life, you may write about it, give lectures, or share wisdom online. In yoga, you may venture ever deeper and eventually emerge with profound insights to share. Practice long enough, and you'll have an experience that will change you and your practice forever. You may determine that the gift is too big to keep to yourself. That is the path of the yoga teacher.

There are as many ways to do yoga poses and sequences as there are yoga teachers out there. If you haven't already, find a teacher whose style works for you, keeps you safe, and helps you grow. The selection of a yoga teacher is a personal one, and you have to find one (or more) that fits you. I've had the good fortune of learning from master teachers, and I've also had my share of teachers whose cues just didn't work for me. Now that I'm a teacher myself, there are some cues that I flat out don't agree with and don't think anyone should be using. I was in a class not so long ago where the teacher actually told us that our legs should be perfectly straight in Seated Forward Fold, and to "reach for those toes!" Ugh, not good—but we'll get to that in a minute.

So, in this section, I'll take you through a small sampling—some tasty "appeteasers" if you will—of my own methods of teaching that, when I learned them, revolutionized my practice. I wanted to include them in this book for one big reason: if you're uncomfortable, or worse, injured in yoga, you won't be able to establish a truly deep practice and ultimately reap the many benefits. We certainly won't be going into all the detail I could offer here, simply because I think for you to get the most out of a teacher's cues, you really should attend a live class or play a video rather than read about them. But having these basic tips as tools in your toolkit will help you when you do get to attend those classes, whether mine or anyone else's.

Consider these an offering, and nothing more than that. As in any yoga class, the cues and adjustments that your teacher gives you are just suggestions. They are invitations for you to explore what works for you. Even more important than learning the movements and postures in your asana practice, is learning how to be mindful of the sensations in your body. The ultimate challenge is to not let ego win over mindful movement. Never let the idea of how the pose "should" look overrule your careful exploration of how and if the pose works for you.

ARRIVAL

There are so very many ways to "arrive" on your mat. However you go about it, I do think that it's an important step to leave the world behind and signal to your body and mind that you're now in the realm of your practice. If you haven't already experienced it, it's difficult to describe the "click" that happens in that moment. It's a settling in, and an automatic shift.

∞ **Meditation:** A short meditation is a beautiful way to arrive in the present moment, take the time to set an intention, and set the tone for the practice that will follow. This could be a seated moving meditation, rotating the torso or seated cat—cow, or arm flows that open and broaden the shoulders. Or it could be a moment of stillness to check in, state your intention, and get ready to flow.

∞ **Top of the mat ritual:** As I described earlier in this book, I have a routine. I didn't try to set it—it just came into being over time—but now it's a signal to my body and nervous system that I'm stepping out of the world for a while and going within. Whether I'm about to start a class taught by one of my master teachers, or do a flow of my own, I often open with my arms sweeping up into a tall, reaching Mountain Pose, then slowly bring my hands, in prayer, in front of my heart. I align my toes, lift up onto the balls of my feet, and set my heels back down. I begin.

∞ **Downward Dog (Adho Mukha Svanasana), Standing Forward Fold (Uttanasana), or Child's Pose (Balasana):** Starting practice in a meditative pose (even an active one like Downward Dog) is a powerful arrival method. Stretching in Downward Dog, pressing the hands into the ground while the hips move up toward the sky, or resting the forehead on the ground in Child's Pose, or hanging toward the toes with knees bent in Uttanasana brings blood flow to the brain and signals that it's time to get your yoga party started.

WARMING UP

There's certainly more than one way to warm up. The first two are pretty obvious: warm the room, or move the body until it gets warm. Either way, heat is created and the body is made ready for the expansive work of stretching and strengthening.

I'm personally not a fan of warming the room in order to warm the body. First, I'm in my fifties, folks; hot flashes are part of this magical time of life, and if you touch the thermostat to raise it above 75 degrees, we will have words. But even before now, as I've been practicing yoga for many years, I didn't enjoy it. Not knocking it, but it wasn't for me. I prefer movement and breath to warm the body. But it's definitely an option, and there are plenty of studios that offer hot yoga.

Aside from the heat in the room making me just plain uncomfortable, another issue I have is dehydration. Having wound my way through the wilderness of an autoimmune disease, I know what my body needs to be well. Hydration is at the top of the list. If you practice yoga in a hot room and sweat balls for an hour and a half, you will, even if you take sips of water throughout the class, emerge dehydrated. There might be some lightheadedness that comes with it; that wouldn't be surprising. So, if you do choose to practice this way, please take care of yourself and drink plenty of water before, during, and after.

Important note on flexibility: Hydration matters A LOT. I had no idea this was actually a thing until a couple of years ago. I thought flexibility was what you get when you stretch a lot. And yes, you can certainly become more flexible over time, no doubt. But when I changed my diet to include at least 96 ounces of water a day, I became way more flexible—and it didn't seem to matter how much I practiced yoga. A little, or a lot, as long as I was hydrated every day, I would stretch and get deeper into stretches very early into practice.

The more common way to warm up is through movement. In Vinyasa classes, for example, Sun Salutations are often done at the start of the class to create warmth in the body. It is also meditative at the start of the practice, setting the stage by flowing through familiar rhythmic movements with the breath.

It's important during the early part of practice to remember that you aren't warm yet. So, if you're in a flow class that's moving along at pace, don't slam your body into poses; instead, take it easy and remember to *feel your way*. With each repetition, breathe deep, and go just a little deeper. You'll get to the stretching and deeply opening poses later.

There's one more way to warm the body, and it's not widely used: the breath. You won't end up breaking a sweat here, but you can create warmth and get stretched even without doing warm-up sequences. Consciously and mindfully, we can open up the tissues by breathing deeply "into" them, expanding them. A great deal of flexibility is actually in the mind—well, the mind–body, meaning that, the body reacts in a certain way because of the subconscious.

Muscles know how to protect themselves. They stay tight when you try to stretch them so that they don't get overstretched. They don't "trust" you yet. When you're moving to warm the body, you're also training the muscles that it's okay to open up; they aren't going to be injured. Each progressive movement "wakes" them up and gets blood flowing into them, and that contracting they do as a defense starts to wane. You can actually replicate this with breath as you stretch. It helps to visually imagine the fibers of the muscle you're stretching opening up in all directions, as you breathe big, slow, deep breaths. As you do so, the muscle fibers realize that they aren't going to be harmed, and they start to release.

MAKING SPACE IN STANDING POSES

You'll often hear alignment cues for standing poses, and this is where many students start lining bones up with bones, or bones up with walls or the floor. For example, take Warrior II. The front knee is bent, back leg straight, back foot not necessarily parallel to the back of the mat, hips open to the side. Gaze is forward, arms are outstretched over the legs. How much you bend that front knee is up to you—it doesn't have to be parallel to the floor (if you hear that, it's just a suggestion). If you're comfortable with your knee going forward a little past your ankle, that's okay too (you may be told to line your knee up directly over your ankle). But the more important things to remember are not if you're making perfect angles; rather, how do your ankle and front knee *feel?* Pressing the knee gently out away from your center line may help make it more comfortable, but you may also need to back up out of the pose, reducing the bend in the knee. Protect that knee, and don't let the idea of a perfect right angle get in the way.

Let's move from Warrior II to Warrior I. Front knee still bent (to whatever degree feels good). Hips turn toward the front of the mat (not necessarily perfectly squared to the front), and the back foot is now at a smaller angle, but not necessarily at a perfect 45-degree angle. Arms go up toward the sky. There's a lot going on here, but it's still common to be passive in this pose. Fire it up and protect your lower back at the same time by pressing the hip attached to your back leg forward toward the front of the mat. You'll get a big ol' stretch in the hip flexor and thigh while lengthening the lower back. Now, you can reach up toward the sky and press your chest forward and up away from the back foot. The same principles apply in high lunge and low lunge, making a big difference in the quality of stretch that you get and the expansiveness that you feel.

Triangle is a pose that causes many students to round the spine to the side as they attempt to put their body in the shape that they see their teacher doing. But if your flexibility isn't there yet, or your anatomy doesn't allow it, here's how to get into the pose. First, with feet wide apart, shift the hips toward the back foot. It's a similar motion to when you're standing on both feet normally and then shift all the weight into one hip: that hip kicks out to the side. That's the same action you want in Triangle. Deeply bend the front knee (this is the part that will really get you where you want to go). The idea is for the torso to be flat, so that you don't pull the side waist or low back. With the leg bent, at least at first, you can get your thigh bone closer to your pelvis, and as you tilt, you'll get the angular version of the pose. Now with your bottom hand on your shin or foot, start to pull the femur up into the hip bone, and the leg will start to straighten as you pull the hips away from the front foot. Leave it bent if it needs to be. Unfurl your arms, spreading them wide like an eagle, turning your chest up toward the sky—the hips and head will reach away from each other as you get long in every direction.

BALANCING

Balance is a crazy thing. It can change from day to day and from side to side. When you balance on your right leg, it might be so solid that you don't wobble at all, and you'd swear your foot has roots and you're one with the big beautiful Earth. Then you flow through the sequence and end up in the same balancing pose on the other side, and it's like your left foot has no brain in it at all, while your arms are flailing madly trying to keep you upright and not take out the students next to you like a bunch of bowling pins. Why is that? Lots of environmental and physiological factors can affect balance, but the biggest cause? Distractions and confidence. It's your head. For whatever reason, at that moment, it may not have been screwed on straight.

The importance of the Drishti cannot be overstated. If you believe you're going to fall over, you're going to fall right out of the pose. If you do, that's okay, get right back in it. But be sure to find a gaze point on the wall or the floor in front of you and hold it the entire time you're balancing. Focusing the mind on one point keeps the mind there and prevents it from wandering around finding all kinds of thoughts to be distracted by.

Let's do the next set of poses in a flow. Stretching into Warrior III, you stand on one leg while the other reaches out behind you, and the arms stretch forward so you're making a letter "T" shape. This can be a wobbly one, but find a Drishti and hold it, while reaching as far forward with the hands as possible as they press away from the back foot, which in turn presses away from the fingertips with the foot flexed. The stretching of the two endpoints away from each other is stabilizing. After a few big breaths, you can draw the top leg's knee into the chest as you come to a standing position, then place the foot on the inner leg (anywhere that feels good from the ankle all the way up to the thigh), and you're in Tree Pose.　　The key to Tree is to let the weight drop into the standing leg's hip so that it kind of kicks out to the side, which sets the top of the femur into the hip and keeps you stable. Pressing the foot into the thigh and the thigh into the foot will help you stay steady. Find that Drishti again. A couple of breaths later, grab a hold of the big toe and stretch the foot straight out in front for Standing Big Toe Pose,　　again letting the top of the femur settle into the hip socket. Let the top leg stay bent as it stretches straight out in front of you. A common thing to do here is to keep the leg straight and round the back so that the foot can be held, but you can pull your back doing that. Keep the leg bent, and let it stay as bent as it needs to be as you press the foot out away from you, keeping your torso upright. Focus your yogi laser on that Drishti. Continuing the balancing cycle, bend the knee deeply and sweep the leg behind, changing the hand position so that you're holding the ankle, thumb up.

Stretch the other arm out front, and you're in Dancer's Pose.　　Many students let the top leg pull them to the side as the leg kicks back, but I encourage you to press your shoulder toward the front and press the hip attached to the top leg in the same direction—to the front. This pose is a backbend (front-body opener) not a side bend, and it's meant to stretch the shoulder and open the front body. Press the foot into the hand and it will start to lift up toward the sky, but there's no need to do a split here. Just keep that Drishti in your sights and breathe.

STRENGTH

I had a shoulder problem for a long time; turns out, it was because I was doing Chaturanga wrong. But according to the cues I'd heard up to that point, I was doing it right. The problem arose when I tried to get my elbow to be directly over my wrist, and to lower myself down so that I was making a perfect 90-degree angle with my upper and lower arm bones. In order to make that happen, you have to lean way out in front of you, top-loading your weight, which can be too much—and the shoulder ends up injured. And I did it over and over again. Finally, I learned that it's okay if you don't lower all the way down in Chaturanga, as long as you don't sink in between the shoulder blades. Lower down to where you feel strong, then stop. Also, lining bones up with bones doesn't work for most people, so don't worry about that 90-degree angle or having your elbow over your wrist. As a matter of fact, I highly recommend not doing that. What I do recommend is to press all of the fingertips into the ground, lifting the middle of the palm up slightly; that grip gives you control. As you lower down, pay attention to the area between the shoulder blades, and keep the hips up; don't let either of them sink. The knees can be lowered to the ground, but that changes which muscles get used in the arms and chest so you don't quite get the same strengthening benefits—but you have to go with what feels good in your body.

In Chaturanga, just as in our next pose, Plank, press your head and heels away from each other in a powerful line. It's stabilizing and strengthening, allowing you to lower down further in Chuturanga, and hold Plank longer.

HIPS

Eoin Finn deserves credit for several of my "Aha!" moments in yoga, and Pigeon Pose is no different. For many years, I would just drop into Pigeon, my back leg stretched out long, my front leg at a right angle, knee and ankle aligned. I would step into it by kicking my front foot behind my opposite wrist, then slam my knee down to the ground, hips on the ground as well. Then I'd immediately fold forward, getting as low as I could go. My left hip was a mess. Whenever I entered this pose, I would hear a "clunking" sound as something shifted in that hip, and it didn't feel good. But I did it anyway, chalking it up to just my anatomical weirdness. Wrong. But I didn't realize until teacher training, when Eoin asked us to stay up high before going into Pigeon, hips off the ground, the front foot tucked in somewhat closer to the hip than I was used to. Then he said, "Before you lower down, pull the hips back, and THEN start to go down." I did that movement, and as I did so, it pulled my front foot further away from my hip and I got an awesome stretch. But not only that, it was a higher-quality stretch—and no clunking sound! I've been doing it that way ever since; it's a totally different pose, and my hip is super happy.

KEEPING THE LOWER BACK LONG

Next, I'll group some poses together to stress the importance of pressing the chest away as a means of keeping the lower back long and safe. Oh, I used to be a back cruncher too, thinking that if I just kept practicing and trying to go deeper, one day I'd be one of those super back-bendy people you see all over Instagram. Then I took one of Bernie's courses and realized I would never be one of them. And I'm okay with that. Here's why. It all depends on how your vertebrae are made and fit together. Remember, all humans are similar, but not the same. My vertebrae may stick out further than yours, so when I enter a backbend, they bump up against each other and stop me from going any further. If I press, I could injure myself, because it's bone meeting bone. But if yours are smaller, when you go to do a backbend, you might have a back that can achieve a much deeper angle. So please pay attention to what you feel back there, and don't push through any pain or pinching. What you're shooting for isn't the deepest expression of a backbending pose, but the healthiest expression of the pose for your own body.

In Cobra, Upward Dog, and Wheel Pose, be sure to press the chest away from the feet, which will keep the lower back long. A great visual is to imagine you're pulling your chest through your shoulders. Also, only do Wheel if you're strong enough to press up into it. If you have a less than bendy back, like me, it helps to put the feet under the hips and come up onto the balls of the feet as you press up, as that gives your back more space. Then you press your chest up and away. In any other backbend (a better name is "front body opener," since the point is not to bend the back but to open the front body), do the same: press the chest away.

It may surprise you that I have the same advice for forward folds. Only this time, you're pressing the chest away from the hips instead of the feet. In all forward folds, press the chest away from the hips as the hips press back—this keeps the lower back long and stops you from pulling it. If you find yourself rounding the spine, lift up, keeping the low back long, and start to press *forward*, not down. In

Seated Forward Fold, bend the knees instead of the back and sit up tall. Keep the lower back long, and press the hips back. As the chest presses away from the hips, you'll notice a totally different quality of stretch. Remember that yoga teacher I mentioned at the beginning of this chapter? She told us to keep the knees locked and reach for the toes, and almost every single person in that class had a rounded spine. They were trying to grab their toes and pull their noses down toward their legs, all of them in a position to easily pull their backs. Bending the knees and pressing the chest forward builds the pose up in a much safer way and actually provides more progress over time, as the stretch is a much higher quality. Once you've got a nice long spine, you press the hips back, and there you'll find an amazing stretch. Same for Pyramid.

It's not about getting your chin on your shin, but pressing the chest down toward the foot as the hip presses up toward the sky.

The chest is also critical in Side Bends. I used to get a strange sharp tweaking in my lower back when bending to the side, especially when I bent over to the right. Then one day, in a class, my teacher took the wrist of my top hand, then pressed my upper back forward while gently pulling my wrist up and back. As I re-bent into the pose, it was completely different. Turning the heart up toward the sky creates a safe way to open the side waist. Do this in all side bends, and your lower back will thank you.

Finally, here are a few recommendations for you, the writer. I've been working at a desk job for over thirty years, so I know what your shoulders feel like. A robust yoga practice will help greatly, but here are a few poses to make sure you work into your practice to really open those areas that get crunched when sitting for long hours.

First, Anjanyasana (Low Lunge). Press into the hip of your back leg, sending it forward to lengthen that hip flexor. These get super contracted when we sit for long periods, so let it get long. Bonus: stretch the arms up and back to release the shoulders. Puppy Pose is essential for releasing the trapezoid muscles, which are the primary source of shoulder pain for writers and desk workers. And Camel Pose puts the body in the opposite position from sitting, with the hips pressed forward, the front body open, the throat open, and shoulders rotated and stretching back. You guessed it: as you press the hips forward, the chest presses away from the feet, up and away.

It can be difficult, especially in a live class, to adapt poses for yourself. But make a commitment to never let your ego win, and to not worry about what everyone else is doing. Every single student in a yoga class is in a different place in their practice. Not only that, their anatomies are all different from yours, and different from each other. So, while one may go (bang!) straight up into the deepest Wheel Pose you ever saw, be bold and stick with Bridge Pose if your shoulders aren't feeling up to Wheel that day. A home practice with online classes makes it a little easier to keep it real, so play around with poses and find what works for you.

There are not only many more poses to get into, of course, but there are also so many ways to adapt poses to your needs—too many for our purposes here. We'll dive way deeper into all of that and much more in our online classes and workshops, should you choose to join me.

PART II

INK MEETS ASANA

Merging the Wisdom of the Ancient

Now that we've explored the foundations and best practices of both yoga and writing, it's time to get into how we'll create a sustainable, powerful unified practice from these two ancient practices. I'm sure you've noticed how much interweaving, blending, and blurring of lines there are between the two. Here, we'll take a look at yoga's role in writing, and how writing can enhance your yoga practice.

In Chapter 1, we learned that yoga is defined not only as "union" but as "remembering," as in, remembering who we truly are—our natural state of wholeness, peace, and connection to something larger than ourselves. As we apply our yoga to writing, think of the possibilities in the expansion of this idea. For it is in the writing where you will find true remembering—true self. You are not the events that have happened to you. But as you write about them, you'll write about you, and you'll find that it's in the remembering where your vision becomes clearer as your heart learns to see. This is where self-discovery lives.

Together, the two practices will create a transformation ecosystem for you to feel physically expansive and free while exploring avenues for growth and discovery. Perhaps most importantly, the combined practice will give you a fresh look at your life and your inner world, reframing your past with more kindness, and setting you up for a thriving and peaceful future. And who knows, perhaps you'll seed the garden of future writing success, as you let bloom the yogi and author within.

12

FIND YOUR FLOW
Freedom in Writing

My inner critic was strong. A total bully, and a real loudmouth who'd
beat me up on a regular basis. Which is strange, because I always considered myself someone who didn't really care what people thought. I
always went my own way, forging a path that was atypical and, let's face
it, super weird at times. My family is filled with a long line of women
who are strong and opinionated, and who know their own mind. Our
edges may be a little hard, but they're not sharp. We know what we
know, but are still able to admit it when we have something to learn;
we're open to growth. And so, I thought I was freer in mind than most,
—enlightened if you will, in my way.

But the loudmouth would sometimes shut me down when it
came to creativity. A stand-out in my family, I was the wild one, the
one who didn't follow the rules. Why? I don't know—maybe because
I'm the youngest sibling, maybe I inherited it from someone else in the
family, or maybe I'm just a pain in the ass. Regardless, I'm allergic to
popular things. For as long as I can remember, I've been repulsed by
stuff that lots of other people like: music, TV shows, movies, clothing,
a socially acceptable life path. Not to intentionally be different; I'm
just… different. When I was young, it bothered me, but not enough to

conform. Now, I embrace it, love it, and glory in my oddities. I mean, we're all weird underneath it all; some of us just hide it better than others. It's part of what makes me do stuff like this—up and write a memoir, then write a memoir/non-fiction book about writing the memoir. It's not what you'd necessarily think of as "normal" behavior. Artists and writers are compelled, called to their craft. It doesn't mean we're the best at it—it just fulfills a need to create. If someone doesn't like your work? Whatever. It's your path and your vehicle, and it's the *doing* that makes it worthwhile.

Even when it came to my painting, I felt like I was pretty liberated in my understanding of expression and "who cares if it's good" attitude. Then someone would say something like, "If art isn't totally lifelike, then it just doesn't seem good to me," and it would stifle my painting practice for a while. But I refuse to engage in that now.

I'd wanted to write for many years. I'd have ideas for stories and discuss them with my mom. She gave me a lot of advice and was very supportive. An avid reader and writer herself, she was wise and intelligent. But her talent was intimidating, and I was insecure and hesitant to begin. Her shadow, though completely unintentional on her part, loomed large. It wasn't until she was gone, and I began writing those letters to her years later, that I was drawn to the keyboard to write our story. And when I sat down to do so, it's like I didn't choose it—I just began. And she was with me every step of the way. It's like we wrote it together.

Years of yoga brought me to that place. It was at the end of a practice that the whisper of a thought first occurred to me, and it was subsequent Savasanas that gave me more and more ideas. I worked my story, so much about my illness and body, through my body and out of my fingertips. The two practices were so intertwined, I can't really refer to them as separate. And writing has become so much a part of me now, I don't think I could stop if I tried. But it was in one conversation, just before I decided to write this book, that was a turning point in me getting over myself.

THE ACCIDENTAL PERFECTIONIST

One day, not too long ago, I had a conversation with a former coworker, who's launched her own professional coaching business. I figured, *I'm doing all right,* and never considered myself someone who needed coaching. But as I was scrolling on LinkedIn, I saw a post by Amanda Riffee talking about her experience with the publishing company through which she'd launched her book, *Unleashing You.* My memoir was getting near the final stages of revision, and I was feeling like I might, maybe, possibly, no not really, okay maybe, submit my manuscript somewhere. So, I thought, let me take a step and just get her perspective on her experience.

We met on a Thursday morning via Google Meet, and it was good to see my former colleague. We caught up a bit, then started talking about my book. I expressed my hesitation with publication, and talked about how I pretty much suck at social media, wondering how I would get my book out there, and could I do it without letting my friends and family know about it? I know—that's a weird thing to ask, and as I said the words out loud, I heard it too. She, kindly, asked why I didn't want anyone I knew to read it (I had no problem with strangers diving into my head, just those I know). And I had to admit, releasing it from my subconscious, why: I didn't want to be judged. Or worse, to fail.

There it was.

We chatted a bit more, and she sent me a Core Motivation Tool (based on the Enneagram, which is a tool for identifying fundamental fears and desires that motivate standard personality types). She said, "Just read each description and let me know which one resonates with you the most. I think I know which one you'll be, but let's see."

So, later that day, I did as she asked—I read each description of fears and desires.

Dammit.

The Perfectionist.

Here I was, in my fifties, having lived my whole life as a person who not only prided herself on self-awareness but had written a memoir where one of the themes was self-discovery through writing. And I'd missed it. I was a perfectionist. How the hell did that happen? Not in the most pure sense—I mean, I'm certainly not a perfectionist in that every detail has to be just so. After all, my mother always said my motto was "good enough." But when I'm passionate about something—my work, my hobbies, my relationships—I can be very hard on myself. It's never "good enough." As much as I'd like to believe that I'm cool with failure, I SO am not.

Well, hell. Turns out, Amanda is GREAT at her job.

One conversation and she changed my perspective about my book. I resolved to knock that crap off, get over myself, and write whatever the hell I wanted to—and put it out in the world if I so chose.

Why did that work? She got me out of my head, had me *externalize* what was stopping me, then gave me a tool to read about myself. Just goes to show, no matter how much we learn or how much we grow, there's always more work to do. I'd admitted what I never wanted to, and I decided then and there that fear would not dictate my actions any more.

I hope you will do the same. Let's talk about some ways to do that and free your mind from that nagging Perfectionist, full of fear and doubt. Remember Ricky's advice? Let's pop in a playlist, hit play, and let's go!

THE HOMECOMING

Flow is the moment the river forgets the banks, the rocks, the twists, and the turns. It is the sacred surrender where the "I" disappears and the story takes the lead. When we find our flow, we are no longer trying to write, we are being written. This is the state of the Middle of Always—where the clock on the wall ceases to matter because you have stepped into the timeless rhythm of creation itself.

THE SOMATIC INQUIRY:
Go for a walk outside, barefoot if possible. Wiggle your toes in the dirt or the sand, feel the gentle scratchiness of the earth as it hugs your feet. Connect to the delicate Always of nature: the trees swaying, birds chirping, sun shining. It is effortless.

☐ Time for a free-writing exercise. This exercise is all about bypassing your inner critic and allowing your thoughts to flow onto the page without judgment or structure. It's a powerful way to tap into your subconscious and discover ideas you didn't know you had.

    ∞ **Set a timer.** Decide how long you want to write. Even five to ten minutes can be effective when you're just starting out. As you get more comfortable, you can increase the time.

    ∞ **Find a quiet space.** Minimize distractions. Turn off your phone, close unnecessary tabs on your computer, and let anyone around you know you need some uninterrupted time.

    ∞ **Open your writing tool.** Whether it's a pen and journal or a computer, have it open and ready to go.

    ∞ **Start writing, and don't stop.** When the timer starts, begin writing whatever comes to mind. Don't worry about grammar, spelling, punctuation, or making sense. Just keep your pen or fingers moving. If you get stuck, write "I don't know what to write, but

I'll just keep going anyway. This exercise is weird, but it seems to be working," or repeat the last word you wrote until a new thought emerges.

∞ **Embrace the mess.** There are no wrong answers. The goal is quantity over quality in this exercise. Don't censor yourself or second-guess. Allow yourself to write about anything and everything – your thoughts, feelings, observations, memories, ideas, even random words.

∞ **When the timer stops, stop writing.** Put down your pen or step away from the keyboard. Take a big breath in, and let it out through an open mouth, making a sound like, "Haaaahhhhh."

∞ **Read it (optional).** You can choose to read what you wrote immediately, later, or not at all. The primary benefit of this exercise is the act of writing itself, not necessarily the finished product. If you do read it, look for surprising ideas or connections, recurring themes, or interesting passages that might spark new inspiration for your more structured writing.

13

INK & ASANA WISDOM
In Daily Life

Yoga teachers are by no means immune to the challenges of living our yoga in daily life. We too are in constant practice. So as I give you advice, please know that I do not speak from a place of perfection or mastery—oh, no, no, no. It's the work that is the path, and we're all on our own version of that path. The same holds true for the cues that we give in the asana practice: we as teachers are very often talking to ourselves, cuing reminders of how to find the pose for our own body that day, in that moment. And so it is true with yoga philosophy: we have to give ourselves constant reminders and bring the practice into daily life. Only then can it become part of us—instinctual actions that we take without trying.

As we've explored, we often think of yoga as what happens during our hour on the mat: the poses, the sweat, the Savasana. And while that's the entry point, it's merely one of the Eight Limbs of Yoga outlined by Patanjali in the *Yoga Sutras.* The true transformative power of yoga unfolds when we begin to integrate its deeper wisdom into each day of our lives. Let's take a look at how the Limbs—the ethical principles, internal disciplines, and practices of concentration—can profoundly enhance your daily interactions, work, relationships, and even your creative process.

BEYOND THE MAT

You've already encountered the concept of "presence" in this book, the act of being fully "here, now." On the mat, this often means noticing the sensations in your body, the rhythm of your breath, or the subtle shifts in your mind. Off the mat, presence becomes an active choice, a conscious application of two other yogic limbs: Pratyahara (withdrawal of the senses) and Dharana (concentration).

Remember, Pratyahara doesn't advise us to shut out the world; it asks us to consciously direct our attention. With continuous notifications and a never-ending flow of tech-enabled information, our senses are constantly bombarded. Pratyahara teaches us to draw our awareness inward, to choose what we engage with and what we let pass. Putting our devices down and unplugging is absolutely the embodiment of this principle. Think of it as developing an internal filter for external noise. For a writer, this might mean turning off notifications while drafting, or consciously stepping away from social media feeds to protect your creative focus. For me, I found that getting away from all that is what actually gave me the time in my day to write. At the same time, it freed me from external influences, so that I could go inside.

In your daily life, it may be the difference between hearing someone speak and truly listening, free from the distraction of your own internal monologue or external stimuli. Ever been scrolling on your phone when someone in the room is talking to you, then you realize you have no idea what they said? Deciding to be present and to listen when they speak, to give yourself the gift of spending time with them, that is Pratyahara.

Dharana, or concentration, builds on this. Once you've minimized sensory distraction, Dharana is the ability to fix your mind on a single point. In asana, this might be your Drishti. In daily life, it's the focused attention you bring to a conversation, a task at work, or even a simple chore.

So, instead of rushing through a meal while scrolling, apply Pratyahara by putting away your phone and focusing on the food itself, **eating mindfully**. Engage Dharana by noticing the colors, textures, aromas, and tastes. How does this simple act deepen your experience of the nourishment you're receiving? Eating in this mindful way allows us to notice when we start to feel full, so that we don't just continue to scoop food into our mouths as we watch TV. It also has the effect of nourishing relationships, as when we're free from distractions, we can enjoy not just the food but the company as well.

In conversations, practice Pratyahara by **actively listening**, resisting the urge to formulate your response while the other person is speaking. Listen to really hear; don't listen to speak. Apply Dharana by focusing solely on their words, tone, and body language. You'll find your understanding deepens and your responses become more authentic and less reactive. To this day, I have much more vivid memories of my grandmother because of this practice; I was truly present in our conversations in her last years.

In a world where multitasking is revered, **choose one important task** and dedicate your full, uninterrupted attention to it. Turn off email alerts, silence your phone, and dive deep. Notice how your efficiency and the quality of your work improve when your mind isn't constantly fragmented. I may shock you by saying that there's actually no such thing as multitasking. Our brains cannot actually do more than one thing at once. You may pride yourself on switching from one task to the next quickly, but when we do that, our brains have to stop and re-start tasks all over again, which takes more time than if we had completed each task before moving on to the next. Many people highlight multitasking on their resume, thinking that it makes them look more hireable, but instead, try communicating true mastery of your ability to complete many different kinds of tasks by talking about your ability to prioritize and organize your day for maximum efficiency. One task at a time drives productivity. So, as you think about your writing, avoid distractions and focus all of your attention on the work.

Writing becomes a direct extension of Pratyahara and Dharana. When you engage in focused writing, you are naturally withdrawing from external distractions and concentrating your mind on the page. Try a descriptive deep dive. Choose a single object in your environment (e.g., a teacup, a plant, a shadow). Set a timer for five minutes and write only about that object, exploring every detail using all five senses. This is a Dharana exercise for your writing.

In your memoir or stories, consciously write scenes where the character (perhaps you) is fully present. Describe what they're *noticing*—the subtle shift in light, the nuanced expression on a face, the underlying tension in a room—to demonstrate, rather than just state, their presence.

Living the Yamas and Niyamas: Your Ethical Compass

Let's revisit the Yamas (ethical restraints) and Niyamas (observances) and how they provide a framework for navigating your interactions with the world and with yourself. To reinforce your knowledge and help them become more automatic, think through some more ways in which you could integrate the Yamas and Niyamas into your life. Here's a list to get you started.

∞ **Satya and Ahimsa:** Before responding in an emotionally charged conversation, pause and ask yourself: "Is it true? Is it kind? Is it necessary?"

∞ **Brahmacharya and Aparigraha:** Consciously set boundaries around screen time or social media to redirect your energy toward more fulfilling activities. Notice if you feel a compulsive need to check your phone (Aparigraha) and practice releasing that grip.

∞ **Santosha:** Begin or end your day by listing three things you're genuinely grateful for. This cultivates contentment regardless of external circumstances.

∞ **Saucha & Asteya:** Consider the source and impact of what you consume—food, news, entertainment. Does it truly nourish you, or does it deplete you? Are you consuming more than you need?

Writing Enhances Living the Yamas and Niyamas:

Writing is a direct pathway to embodying these principles, offering a space for reflection, accountability, and deeper understanding:

∞ When faced with a decision, journal about it through the lens of the Yamas and Niyamas. "If I apply Ahimsa, what is the most non-harming path here? What does Satya ask of me?"

∞ Free-write about a moment of profound contentment (Santosha). What specific sensory details were present? What thoughts did you have? This practice cultivates gratitude and deepens your capacity for joy.

∞ Use your journal to track your consistent efforts (Tapas) in a particular area of your life or writing. Celebrate showing up, even when the results aren't immediate. This reinforces discipline.

∞ Use your memoir or stories to explore your own relationship (Svadhyaya) with these principles. When did you embody them? When did you struggle? How did those choices shape your experience? This self-study makes the abstract concepts of the Yamas and Niyamas tangible and personal.

Pranayama as a Living Tool: Breathing Through Life's Rhythms

In Chapter 9, we explored pranayama on the mat as a powerful way to regulate your nervous system and prepare for deeper states of awareness. But the power of conscious breath extends far beyond your dedicated practice time. It's a constant, always-available tool for managing stress, enhancing focus, and finding calm in the midst of all those people and events that drive you crazy, creating the daily chaos that is life.

Your breath is intimately linked to your emotional state. When you're stressed or anxious, your breath often becomes shallow and rapid. When you're calm and relaxed, it's slow and deep. Reverse that by breathing slowly and deeply in an intentional way, and relaxation will follow. By consciously manipulating your breath, you can directly influence your nervous system, shifting from a state of fight-or-flight to one of rest-and-digest:

∞ Before a challenging conversation, during a stressful work moment, or when you feel overwhelmed, take three slow, deep breaths. Inhale deeply through your nose, letting your belly expand, and exhale slowly through your mouth or nose. Counting can help: inhale for a count of four, exhale for a count of six. Even thirty seconds can cause a meaningful shift.

∞ Use your breath to mark transitions throughout your day. Before starting a new task, take a few deep breaths to clear your mind. Try breathing deeply into the belly, letting it relax and get full, then bringing the breath up into your chest, and all the way up into the shoulders.... then sigh that out through an open mouth: Haaaaaa. Before leaving work, take a few breaths to release the day's stress, and leave it behind.

∞ When you need to concentrate, try Box Breathing (Sama Vritti) for a few rounds (inhale for a count of four, hold for four, exhale for four, hold for four). This rhythm can sharpen your mental clarity.

∞ If you find yourself in an emotionally intense situation, use your breath as an anchor. Focus on a slightly longer exhale to signal to your nervous system that it's safe to calm down.

Stepping off the mat doesn't mean leaving your yoga behind. It means expanding its reach, allowing its wisdom to permeate every aspect of your life. The Yamas and Niyamas become your ethical compass, guiding your interactions with the world and yourself. Pratyahara and Dharana become your tools for cultivating a deep, unwavering presence amidst distraction. And your breath, a constant companion, becomes a powerful ally for navigating life's inevitable ebbs and flows, ups and downs.

This integration isn't always easy. It demands conscious effort, self-awareness, and a willingness to meet yourself, honestly, in every moment. But as you weave these yogic Limbs into your daily existence, you'll discover a profound sense of authenticity, peace, and resilience that extends far beyond the edges of your yoga mat. Your life itself becomes the most profound yoga practice, and your writing becomes the testament to that ongoing journey of growth, discovery, and **remembering** who you truly are.

THE HERE & NOW

A life and a legacy are not built only in the quiet of the sanctuary; it is tested in the noise of the Tuesday afternoon. The wisdom of the mat and the mirror of the page must eventually leak into the way we hold our tea, the way we speak to a stranger, and the way we breathe through our fatigue. To live your Ink & Asana is to realize that every moment is a potential sentence in the masterpiece manuscript of your life.

THE SOMATIC INQUIRY:

In your next encounter with someone... difficult, let the sound of your heartbeat remind you of a drum. The thrumming becomes drumming, like the beat of the song of your life. That person has only turned up the volume. Thank them and sing a verse about boundaries. Hum along with the bass line. Dance as you walk away.

PUT IT INTO PRACTICE

Now that we're integrating writing and yoga, designing a combined practice, it's worth looking into how you can use your yoga to enhance your writing experience. Reading about yoga philosophies and history is one thing, but writing about weaving them into your practice takes it to the next level. These writing prompts are designed to guide you through these traditional yogic principles, encouraging you to reflect on your aspirations as a writer, from journaling to memoir, and how these ancient teachings can serve as a compass for all of it.

Kindness is something we cultivate in yoga—kindness toward ourselves and others—to create a sustainable way of living this life. Crack open your journal and explore how these principles can shape your conduct and your approach to your writing.

Yamas

☐ **Ahimsa (non-harm):**
  - ∞ How can the principle of non-harm guide your choice of words, your portrayal of others, your portrayal of yourself, and your self-critique in your writing? Consider how

you can write with compassion, even when exploring difficult truths. What impact does self-judgment have on your creative flow?

☐ **Satya (truthfulness):**

∞ How does Satya relate to the authenticity of your voice and the honesty of your narrative? What truths are you eager to explore in your writing, and what fears might arise when committing to total honesty on the page?

☐ **Asteya (non-stealing):**

∞ In what ways might a writer "steal" from themselves (e.g., procrastinating, self-doubt, not giving their full effort)? How can Asteya encourage you to value your own creative time while also not neglecting important relationships?

☐ **Brahmacharya (moderation/right use of energy):**

∞ How does Brahmacharya apply to your writing routine and creative energy? Are you over-writing, under-writing, or scattering your focus? How can you channel your creative energy more mindfully to sustain your writing practice?

- ☐ **Aparigraha (non-possessiveness / non-greed):**
    - ∞ As a writer, are you overly attached to perfection, external validation, or specific outcomes for your work? How can Aparigraha help you release these attachments, allowing your writing to flow more freely and joyfully?

Niyamas

- ☐ **Saucha (purity/cleanliness):**
    - ∞ How can Saucha apply to your writing environment and your mental space when you write? What habits or mental clutter might you clear away to create a purer, more focused creative process?

- ☐ **Santosha (contentment):**
    - ∞ Do you find yourself constantly striving for an unreachable ideal in your writing or comparing your work to others? How can Santosha help you find contentment and appreciation for your current stage of writing, wherever you are, celebrating progress rather than solely focusing on perceived shortcomings?

- [ ] **Tapas (discipline/fire):**
    - ∞ Tapas is focused effort fueled by passion. What disciplined practices can you commit to in your writing (e.g., daily word count, dedicated writing time) that will help get rid of obstacles and bring you closer to your goals?

- [ ] **Svadhyaya (self-study/study of sacred texts):**
    - ∞ Writing *is* Svadhyaya. How can your writing become a primary tool for self-study, allowing you to explore your thoughts, feelings, and experiences with curiosity and honesty? Consider how reading about writing, different literary styles, or philosophy also contributes to this practice.

- [ ] **Ishvara Pranidhana (surrender to a higher power/higher self):**
    - ∞ Do you wrestle with control over your creative process, your audience's reception, or the final outcome of your work? How can Ishvara Pranidhana encourage you to surrender to the flow of inspiration, trust the writing process, and release attachment to results?

By working through these prompts, you're not just practicing yoga or writing in isolation. You're creating a unified practice—a synergistic relationship where each discipline informs and enhances the other. Your yoga practice provides grounded wisdom, and your writing provides the space for active reflection, integration, and articulation. Let your pen be an extension of your intention, your time on the mat an extension of your written exploration.

14

A BLENDED PRACTICE
Beyond the Blank Page

Writing, like yoga, is a practice of unraveling. Just as tension lives in our body's tissues, stories live in the deep corners of our mind, body, and spirit. Writing is about stripping away the layers of expectation, fear, and self-criticism to reveal the unique story waiting to emerge. This chapter will guide you through practical techniques to access that raw, unfiltered voice, turning your thoughts, past, and experiences into prose that's alive with the essence of you.

The following exercises will help you get into the right headspace as you get ready to write, or if you've tried to get started but had trouble keeping up with it. Before you begin, there are a few things to check off your list. First, make the commitment to the practice. Habits take time to create. Ever started a workout regimen and did great for a few days or a week, but then just stopped? The main reason is that it didn't become a *habit*—because you didn't give it enough time. It's not a failing on your part, nor a problem with your willpower. What you didn't do was give it the time it needed to become a habit. It takes something like twenty-eight days of engaging in an activity for it to transform into a habit. And when it does, it becomes automatic, and you won't have to try so hard. When I'm in a daily yoga and writing practice, I don't have to choose to do either. I just show up on my mat, and I show up at the keyboard, every day. More often, I have to choose to give myself a break and take a day off.

So, make the commitment to a daily yoga and writing practice—for a month. Start with that, and let it become habit. Work both into your daily routine (I'll give you a strategy for this later in the book).

Work through the rest of this chapter as the way into your integrated *Ink & Asana* practice. Take the time to prepare the body and mind, set some ritual to your beginning, and it will become a part of your every day, and a part of you, very soon.

YOGA INSPIRED PRE-WRITING RITUALS

Just as you prepare your body and mind for a yoga session, mindful preparation can transform a writing session. These rituals aren't rigid rules, but simply a way of creating a bridge from your daily life to your creative space. It's your "arrival." Make a selection from the list below to try—but I bet you end up coming up with your own interpretation, or sequence that speaks to you:

Before sitting down to write, engage in a short breathwork (Pranayama) practice. This signals to your nervous system that it's time to shift into the present moment. Choose one of these, or another pranayama of your choice:

∞ **Two-Part Breathing:** Let all of the air in your lungs out through an open mouth. Inhale slowly through your nose, letting the air fill your belly first, then your chest. Hold the breath for a beat, then slowly exhale, letting the air leave your chest first, then your belly. Repeat three to five times.

∞ **Box Breathing (Sama Vritti):** Inhale for a count of four, hold for four, exhale for four, and hold for four. Repeat five to seven times.

∞ **Alternate Nostril Breathing (Nadi Shodhana):** As described in Chapter 3, this balancing breath can harmonize the left and right hemispheres of your brain, fostering both logical thought and creative flow. Practice for two to three minutes to clear mental clutter.

A few minutes of simple asanas and gentle movement can release the physical tension that often accompanies mental blocks, and just helps us transition the mind out of the rest of the day and into writing practice time:

∞ **Downward Dog:** There's something about Downward Dog that just resets the mind, letting blood flow to it, flipping the world upside down. Press your hands, shoulder-width apart, into the ground as your hips stretch up to the sky. Knees can be bent, heels up if you're not feeling open. In an upside-down "V" shape, breathe deeply.

∞ **Cat-Cow:** A way to open the mid-body both front and back, Cat-Cow is as much a breathing exercise as it is movement. On your hands and knees, arch your spine, lifting the crown of the head and the hips toward the sky as your chest and belly lower on the inhale (Cow) and deeply round your back on the exhale (Cat).

∞ **Child's Pose:** Rest your forehead on the ground, arms extended or alongside your body, hips to heels (using a cushion if that's not comfortable). This pose is deeply calming and allows you to turn inward, fostering introspection before you begin to write. It also lets us get humble and surrender.

∞ **Seated Spinal Twist:** Sitting cross-legged, gently twist your torso to each side, using one hand on the opposite knee to assist the twist and the other hand behind you to keep the spine long. This can help release tension in the upper back and neck, areas where writers often hold stress.

The opening rituals don't just relax you; especially with repetition, they signal to your subconscious that you're ready to get started, letting the world fall away while you create. It's the runway, your pen or fingers getting ready to fly.

My lightbulb moment, described in a previous chapter, may have resonated with you. Perfectionism is often fear in disguise—fear of not being good enough, fear of judgment, fear of failure. The next exercise combines physical poses with a writing prompt to help you, quite literally, move through this common obstacle. It's designed to cultivate courage and resilience, recognizing that fear is a natural part of the creative process, not a sign to stop. Found something you're scared to write about? Lean in—you've just found the good stuff.

Flow:

∞ **Find your Warrior I (Virabhadrasana I):** Stand with your feet wide apart, front foot facing forward, back foot at a comfortable angle. Connect the ribs and pelvis by engaging the core gently. Press the hip forward, away from your back foot. Bend your front knee until it's at a comfortable but challenging level, not necessarily directly over your ankle, keeping your back leg strong. Lift your arms overhead, palms facing each other. Drop your shoulders away from your ears, and spread your fingertips wide.

∞ **Feel the pose:** Notice the strength in your legs, the openness in your chest, the upward reach of your arms. Where do you feel power? Where do you feel vulnerability?

∞ **Acknowledge fear:** In this strong pose, consciously bring to mind a fear associated with your writing (e.g., "My writing isn't good enough," "No one will care about my story," "What if I can't finish this?").

∞ **Breathe into it:** Take three to five deep breaths, directing your inhale into the fear, and your exhale into releasing the grip it has on you.

∞ **Release it:** Bring your hands down to the ground on either side of your front foot, and step back into a Plank position. Lower down, Chaturanga (strong), and push up into Upward Dog—victoriously breathing in deeply. Flip the feet and lift the hips back into Downward Dog, and let something out of you with a Lion's Breath—stick your tongue out as you exhale. Haaaaaa.

∞ **Repeat on the other side:** Switch legs and repeat the process, bringing a different fear or the same one to mind.

Write:

- ∞ **Return to your writing space.** Keep the feeling of grounded strength from Warrior I.

- ∞ **Write the worst first line you can think of:** Your task is to write the worst possible opening sentence for whatever you're working on, or simply the most cliché, boring, or nonsensical first sentence you can imagine:

  - ∞ *Example (if writing a memoir):* "The sun rose that morning, just like it always did, and I woke up."
  - ∞ *Example (if writing a short story):* "Once upon a time, there was a dude."

- ∞ **Write it:** Write that "ugly" first line down. Don't hesitate.

- ∞ **Continue for five minutes:** Now, without editing or re-reading that first sentence, simply continue writing for five minutes. Let whatever comes out, come out. Don't worry about perfection, coherence, or quality. The goal is to bypass the inner critic (loudmouth!) that would have stopped you at the first sentence and simply get words on the page.

- ∞ **Reflect:** After five minutes, read what you've written. What did you notice? Did the "ugly" first line truly stop you, or did words flow despite it? This exercise helps you realize that the act of writing, even imperfectly, is always possible. The fear is often louder than the actual challenge.

By intentionally creating space for both the physical and emotional aspects of your being, and by challenging the need for immediate perfection, you'll cultivate a deeper connection to your authentic voice, allowing it to just come out and let your unique story unfold.

Great story happens when you can feel the author's experience not through a description of the feeling, but through a description of the experience that evoked the feeling. This is why journaling is so important as a first exercise. Even if you sit down to write your memoir with zero journaling experience, the first drafts of the essays that will become your narrative are memories, told from your perspective, just as you would journal about them. Later, you'll turn that essay into a scene.

15

THE ASANA OF MEMORY
The Roadmap to Story

Whether you are embarking on this excavation alone to find and examine your own story or sitting across from a loved one to celebrate a shared history, the structure of memory remains the same. A memoir isn't just a record of what happened; it is a somatic map of how you became the person you are. This roadmap will help you navigate the historic volumes of your past and turn them into a legacy for the future.

I've had countless journals filled with a lifetime of jotted notes and fragments—fleeting moments captured in a private shorthand. You may have the same, and think it was just a venting, a release in the moment. But there's immense potential held within those pages. And even if you've never picked up a journal, there's no time like the present, for you'll embark on a wild journey into your past and come out with a story. And once you've harvested those memories, what comes next? A memory is a seed, but a memoir is the tree that grows from it, with deep roots, reaching branches, and a life of its own.

Your life is not a list of events; it's a living story. The leap from memory to memoir isn't just recounting what happened. The bigger task is discovering what it all means. This chapter will give you the tools to unearth the hidden narrative in your past, turning your personal record into story.

Your story, your life, is singular and unique. But how do you take the seemingly random, chaotic expanse of your memories and turn it into a cohesive narrative? The answer lies in approaching it with the same mindful, deliberate practice you bring to your asana practice: a structured, intentional flow that builds from the ground up. It works its way through laying a foundation, expanding and exploring, challenging with a climax pose, then winding down and letting the body integrate what it's learned. Let your story follow a similar flow.

Here, we'll get into a framework to get you started: from the first whispered memory to the final, polished page. Will you stumble, wobble, and fall over like you did last week when you were trying to balance in Half Moon Pose? You bet you will. Then you'll get right back up, and get back to it, embracing the comedy of you.

In Chapter 4, I described my writing experience—how holding up the mirror that was my memoir changed not just how I saw my story, but how I viewed myself. I was overwhelmed with forgiveness for the girl, for the young woman on those pages who'd made decisions, and the older one who'd become mysteriously ill. I forgave myself for living a life full of decisions, and no longer saw them as mistakes. I forgave myself for not wanting anyone to know I was sick. I forgave myself, most surprisingly, for getting sick in the first place.

Something else I never expected, I learned that grief isn't a "bad" thing, or something to get over. Before I wrote that book, I was convinced I had a handle on my grief. It had settled into my bones and would just reside there, humming low. I thought the initial trauma had receded, that the weight of absence had settled into a manageable ache.

I was wrong.

What began as a private exercise—simple letters to someone who would never read them—became an unstoppable torrent. In just a couple of months, chapters poured out of me. I wrote in the early mornings, at lunch time, after work, in the evening in between dinner and relaxing. I wrote on the weekends, on airplanes, whenever I could find the time. I paused all participation in social media, because ick, anyway. It was an addiction to the eviction of thoughts and emotions that had been marinating inside me for years. It was an act of putting my story through the wash, of taking the grief that had settled in my bones and letting my fingers on the keyboard articulate what my heart couldn't.

Through the writing, I vomited out all the things I was too afraid to talk about. And once it was done, the writing stopped, because wow. An avalanche of inner stuff had fallen out, and I was left with a need to heal. As I shifted my diet back to the optimal one that I knew would bring healing, I slowly started to feel physically and emotionally well again. I gave myself the time to find rest and healing. But eventually, I returned to the work, listening to the little whisper in the back of my mind—and I started picking up the bits and pieces in revision, rinsing them in the clarity that I'd been given by it all.

The grief, I discovered, hadn't vanished—not that I'd expected or really wanted it to. It's still there, a part of me, but it's changed, and it's no longer in control. By owning my story, I vanquished its power. What once felt like a wound has become a sacred part of my history. I love my grief. It's a warm hug that I can allow myself to feel from time to time. My grief is sweet memory, time travel, and it has become a form of immense gratitude and a celebration of a beautifully full life.

The biggest revelation? Writing didn't just help me release the loss of my mother; it helped me realize how present she still is. Through the act of writing, I saw that my heart has a way of "seeing" that provides the clearest vision in remembering. In that process, it was as if we were writing together, a connection I never knew I was missing.

Now, I'm hooked. The act of writing is a gift, a way to process our lives and give our stories a voice. It's an act of love, for ourselves and for those we're writing about, and writing for. And I believe that by sharing my story, my experience, it may help at least one other person begin to write their own. I hope that person is you. I encourage you to put your own bits and pieces out into the world, and in so doing, put your story through the wash. It will emerge changed, and so will you.

Let's begin.

PHASE 1: THE JOURNALING PRACTICE

We'll start with pre-work. As you embark on the journey of writing your memoir, there are a few things to consider. These tips will guide your journey, so before you even start to think, "What is the plot of my story?" or, "What memories will I include?" you'll want to take some time to journal about where you're going with this project.

First, think about your "**why**." There are many reasons to write a memoir, and many different potential audiences for your work. You may want to write it only for yourself, to enhance your analysis of your past experiences and gain perspective. That is an excellent reason in and of itself. Most people think that writing a book means that you intend to have it published, but that's not necessarily the case. Turning journal entries into a memoir is a powerful experience, but it doesn't mean that you have to show it to a single soul.

You may want to write it for your family. There may be significant stories you wish to share, to leave a legacy. Or maybe you've dealt with a chronic illness or other challenge in your life, and you want to give your family the benefit of your experience so that they can learn from it.

Then, of course, you may wish to eventually publish your work and share it with the world. But today, you may not be sure, and that's perfectly okay. Sometimes, it takes getting into the writing of it before you can even think about what you're going to do with it. That's how it was for me. It started as a tool for me alone, then it became something I wanted to share with family, then it evolved beyond that. It's good to start thinking now about who you're writing for, so that you can write directly for that audience. But if it evolves over time, you can address the changes in the revision process, turning it into something for an audience broader than your original intention.

Next, take some time to journal about your **motivation**. The events of your life, or part of your life, may make a compelling story, but behind that, what's really fueling your desire to write it? Is it outrage or anger? An expression of joy? A way to process grief? A desire to help others? To take your power back? To effect social change? Memoir is a vehicle for your voice, so what is it that you want to say? What's your primary message and motivation for getting started?

Once you've taken some time to journal and explore the why and for whom, and you're ready to dive in, you need raw material. And I mean raw. Think of your initial journaling as a gentle warm-up, a way to unfurl your tightly wound ego and bathe in the anecdotes of your past. Don't worry about plot, theme, or even good grammar at this stage. The goal is simply to get your memories onto the page, unedited and uncensored. Bring it.

Start with simple prompts. Don't think big, like "my whole life story." Think small. What's the earliest memory you have? What's a smell that instantly transports you back in time? Describe the view from your childhood bedroom window. What was the first place you ever traveled to on your own? For me, I wanted to write memories of my time with my mom and grandmother. I started jotting those memories down—the ones that stood out—and as soon as I started, more started knocking on the door wanting to be written as well.

Lean into the physical. What did the air feel like on that day? What was the texture of the fabric of the sweater you wore? What did the food taste like? The more sensory details you can capture, the richer your raw material will be. This is where your "show, don't tell" begins its slow, quiet work. In the first drafts, and especially in the journaling phase, don't worry too much about this—but if you can work it in from the beginning, then great.

Don't judge; just write. This isn't anywhere near a final draft. It's an exercise in memory retrieval. If a memory feels insignificant, write it down anyway. Sometimes, the smallest moments hold the key to a larger truth. Allow your hand to move freely across the page, capturing snapshots of your life without worrying about their place in the larger narrative.

PHASE 2: THE DIGITAL SANDBOX

Once you have a collection of memories, it's time to start organizing them. This is where you may bring digital tools into the practice. Apps designed for brainstorming and organization like Miro or Trello (I used Jamboard, and when that was discontinued I switched to Lucid), or even just a simple note-taking app like Notion or Evernote, can be your digital "sticky notes." Each note represents a scene, a memory, or an important event. If you want to work with paper instead, grab some index cards and use those. The idea is that you want to jot down a memory on each one, and then you'll need a medium that will allow you to move them around, find patterns, and group them by color.

∞ Go through your journal entries and distill each distinct memory into a single "note" if you think it's a significant event or a scene that might move the story along. Give it a title. For example: "The Smell of My Grandmother's Kitchen," "First Day of High School, 1988," "Walking the Streets of Key West."

∞ At first, just dump them all onto a virtual canvas. Don't try to order them. This is your pile of building blocks.

∞ Now, start to look for connections. Drag and drop the notes around. Do two memories belong in the same chapter? Does a series of memories show a clear progression, like learning a new skill or navigating a difficult relationship? You might discover that a memory from your childhood and one from your adult life share a common emotional thread. Group them together. As I worked, I started to see themes: groups of memories of Mom taking care of me when I was sick, me trying to take care of her when she was diagnosed, the progression of my illness, of hers, and the interweaving threads of stories she told me about our family history.

∞ Use colors or tags to categorize your notes. You might have categories for "turning points," "character introduction," "conflict," or "moments of insight." In this process, you're seeing the lines of force and energy in your story. My colors helped me easily see each component and theme: letters, her taking care of me, me taking care of her, us taking care of Grandma, health journey, etc. You're creating the blueprint, the architecture of your narrative. Themes start to emerge, and structure comes into focus.

∞ A great next step here is to write an extremely simple version of your story (perhaps just a paragraph or two). If you were going to write a quickie about the memories you've captured, how would you structure it? What's the synopsis? What would the timeline be? What's the short story? This will help you start to imagine your thoughts and recollections as a story, and determine what your book is really about. It will help you figure out the arc of the story as well.

∞ Think through how the story will make sense for the reader. Often, when dealing with our own memories, we know the story inside and out, so we may think telling the story out of order, or in an artistic way is the best way to go. And while that may be true in some cases, it can often confuse the reader. So be careful, and remember that the audience may know nothing of your story, so you'll want to organize it in a way that will help them understand where you've been and where you're going.

PHASE 3: SCENE AND STRUCTURE

Once you have a rough order for your sticky notes, or whatever brainstorming medium you've decided to use, it's time to create a more formal structure. Remember, a memoir is not a biography. It's not about covering every single year of your life. Matter of fact, I skipped entire decades. It's about a theme, an insight, a particular journey.

To create that structure, you may want to start by identifying the story's **central conflict**. Finding the central conflict in your memoir is like locating the main artery of your story—the underlying tension that drives the narrative forward. It's often not a singular event, but rather an ongoing struggle or question that propels you (the protagonist) through the journey you're recounting. For me, it was facing my illness, and getting through the challenge that forced me to make myself sick in order to get a diagnosis, while dealing with my ongoing grief. Your conflict might be external like mine, such as battling an illness, or it may be overcoming a difficult relationship. As often, it's an internal struggle: grappling with grief, confronting deep-seated beliefs, seeking identity, or striving for forgiveness. Unearthing this core tension gives your memoir its purpose and emotional resonance, transforming a mere recounting of events into a compelling exploration of personal growth and change that will speak to your audience, who will see themselves reflected in your story.

Next, find your **central theme.** Look at your organized notes. What's the story *really* about? Is it about finding your voice? Overcoming an obstacle? The meaning of home? This central theme is your story's spine, the foundation upon which everything else rests. A powerful way to find your story's core is to identify a pivotal moment of change, or the **turning point**. This is the before and after of your narrative, the scene where everything shifts. What were the emotions and thoughts present in that crucial moment?

Every scene or memory you include in your memoir should support your theme, always moving the story forward. It's tempting to include all significant memories or people in your story, because it is, after all, the story of your life. But when writing a memoir, remember that it's not a story about your whole life. It's about a central conflict that you faced and a theme that threads its way through all of your chapters. There may be significant events that you will completely leave out since they don't support the story.

Next, ask yourself what is the **inciting incident**? What is the kick-off for the story you want to tell? For me, in my present day timeline, it was deciding to go through the dietary challenge that would take me back to being ill. For my backstory arc, it was getting sick in the first place. For the story you want to share, what's the thing that happened that started you on the path to change?

In Chapter 10, we discussed the arc of a story. Even though your memoir is the story of your life, it still needs a narrative arc. You might choose a **three-act structure** to give it one. Act I is the setup, where you introduce your world, your younger self, and the central conflict or question that the story will explore. Act II is the confrontation. This is the longest part of the story, where you face challenges and make discoveries—basically, it's where things get complicated. It's the heart of your journey. And in Act III, you take your readers through the resolution. You've changed, you've learned something, and here's where you show the reader the person you've become and the insights you've gained.

Another way to look at it is to identify the opening scene—perhaps this is the stasis (before the events of the story)—then select a few scenes for the middle of the story, which would include the rising action, climax, and falling action. Then select the final scene, the conclusion, the resolution. You'll fill in more around the middle, but identifying those components of the story can help you see the arc. Then ask the important question: "Where did my transformation/change happen, and how?"

If you're beginning at the beginning in a chronological story arc, you might consider making the prologue or first chapter a bit of a teaser that introduces the central conflict before getting into the stasis. If you start all the way back before anything happened with respect to that conflict, the reader may not know why they should read the story. If you tease the conflict, they know a bit of what's coming, and will engage in the backstory in order to get there.

Now it's time to turn your groupings of sticky notes into chapters. Give each chapter a working title that reflects the emotional or narrative content. For example, "Finding Grace" or "Holding On."

Generally, when you shift from journal to memoir writing, the story is no longer for you. It's your story, but it's for your readers. This may feel weird, and admittedly, it's something I had to work through. But even if you ultimately decide not to share it, the journey of writing it in this way is still worthwhile. And if you do decide to share it, just as a new business has to determine who their target customers will be, you'll want to figure out who your readers are. Is it your family and friends only? Or is it the world at large? If you will plan to publish at some point, who, specifically, will be interested in your story? What's their life like, and what do they need to get out of your book? Getting specific about who they are will help you write for them.

PHASE 4: REVISION

Now comes the sculpting, the art. You have your blueprint, your draft, your raw material. But a first draft is just a series of events. Revision is where you breathe life into the story—kind of like the asana of writing, the physical and mental work of refinement.

Before you get started with this next phase, or even at the same time, if you haven't already done so, **read your competition**. Research books on the same topic as yours. Buy a few of them, and give them a read. You'll want to do this for a couple of reasons. Take a look at how they structured the story. Read to look for their voice—how does it speak to you? You'll also want to map how your book will stand out; it may be similar in genre and topic, but how is it really unique?

Be strategic with your content. Take out the trash, i.e., the memories or passages that don't tie in tightly with the narrative. And if you find yourself doing more telling (also known as *exposition*) than showing, you'll want to start to work through how you can weave those facts more deeply into the narrative. Can you put that passage into a scene so that it unfolds for the reader organically? This may also involve throwing out some of your favorite parts of your story. It did for me. I realized that some of what I thought I wanted to say was just me putting everything I remembered into that book. But memoir is about story, not a data dump of your life. You'll have to pull up your big person pants and toss some stuff out. That said, be sure to include everything that's needed to support the story arc and the growth of the main character: you.

But as you're revising your memoir, you'll next want to assess your use of **show, don't tell.** Go through your manuscript line by line. As you read, ask yourself: Am I telling the reader something, or am I showing them?

- ∞ **Telling:** "I was angry."
- ∞ **Showing:** "My jaw tightened. I felt the heat rise from my chest to my face, and my hands clenched into fists in my lap."

To really get into the show, don't tell revision, engage all five senses to create immersive scenes. What did you see, hear, smell, taste, and feel? What was the light like? This is where your journaling practice pays off. These details transport the reader directly into your experience. When recalling a conversation, notice where you feel tension. How does a character's body show what they feel? Don't just write that a character felt sad. Describe the droop of their shoulders, the way they stared at their feet, the quiet sigh that escaped their lips. This is the embodiment of your story.

Try using **revealing dialogue** to avoid telling, instead of showing. But dialogue should do more than just convey information. It should reveal character, advance the plot, and heighten tension. How can you show the reader what a character is like, rather than describing them? Pay attention to how people *actually* speak—their quirks, hesitations, and unique phrasing. Dialogue can be tough, because in memoir, it may feel like you're making it up—and at times you may be. Memoir is not a factual record or historical document; it's a story based on real events. So, you may need to take some liberties with dialogue, since it's unlikely you remember every conversation word for word. Not to mention, if you're using revealing dialogue to help the reader get backstory, you may be completely fabricating some bits.

Vary your sentence length and structure to create rhythm and control the **pacing** of your story. Short sentences can build tension or convey quick action. Longer, more complex sentences can slow the pace, allowing for reflection or detailed description. So mix it up.

As you know by now, the point of memoir is not what happens in the story, but what happens to the author as the story unfolds. It can help to actually draw a visual of how the events affected you, the **arc of your change**, and how you and your life were altered. That's what your readers want to know: all this stuff happened, but how did it affect you? In this process, map each of the scenes you've chosen to include in your story to the impact you're trying to make. Why is the scene included? Why is it important? How does it move the story forward and support the points you're trying to make?

Of course, your **unique voice** is what will make your memoir distinct. Allow your personality to shine through. Is your voice funny, witty, reflective, direct, or poetic? Finding your voice involves writing from the heart, with the same essence of you that you would bring if you were actually speaking.

And finally, try **reading your work aloud**. This is the single most effective way to catch clunky phrasing, awkward sentences, and places where the flow feels off. Your ear is a different kind of editor then your eye—and when you're drafting an entire book, it's easy to get bogged down in the volume of material that you're reviewing. Read something enough in revision after revision, and your eyes will skim right over some stuff. Reading aloud helps you rise up out of the forest, so that you can see the trees.

As you may recall, after I completed my first draft, I walked away. I'm not saying you have to do that for a period of months like I did, but I recommend you take a break. Practice a ton of self-care. Telling your story for the first time can be exhilarating and exhausting. You probably processed, or are in the process of processing, a ton of emotion. Let that stuff marinate and cool down for a while. You'll come back to your book later, clear and ready to scrub those memories with some of the clarity and perspective that you've been given.

Your memoir is a journey of discovery, not just for you, but for your reader. By approaching it with the deliberate structure of a physical practice—from the initial free-form journaling to the careful arrangement of digital notes and the final, refining work of revision—you can transform a collection of memories into a powerful and resonant story. Breathe. Write. Revise.

For me, keeping it simple was everything. Read books about writing for inspiration and guidance on style, but watch out for the overwhelming flood of information that's out there. There are masters of memoir far more talented than me who can help, but I found that when I read too much about writing, I became a bit intimidated, which gave me pause. It's okay to keep it simple, then layer in the expert advice here and there through your revision process.

Stay true to your voice, finding it in the writing if you don't know what it is yet. Memoir is fascinating not because of the events that take place within it. Readers are drawn to you, the author, and what you have to say in your own unique way. No one will tell a story like you; no one has lived your life and experienced those events in your head and heart. Give your reader the gift of coming along with you and learning something about themselves, that they see reflected in you and your story.

The Trail Divergent

A life is not a straight line. It is a series of sacred shapes we have drawn, held in the dark, and unfolded in the light. To map your memoir is to find the alignment in your chaos—to see how the bending of your spirit was actually the shoring up of your spine. You are the cartographer of a territory that only you have traveled, charting a path for those who will one day seek to find their way home to you.

The Somatic Inquiry:

Imagine your life as a series of stops on a long winding trail. Sketch it's path, through mountains, over rivers, in and over rocky ground in deep canyons. Name the chapters of your life as you draw these features on your map. How did one shape the direction in which you explored the next?

PUT IT INTO PRACTICE

Be gentle with yourself.

∞ Writing about difficult memories is an act of courage, and it's okay to take breaks, to write in fragments, and to not have a clear narrative from the start. Think of it as an excavation rather than a construction.

∞ You don't have to write about memories that you don't want to. Don't feel like you need to include everything in your life. You don't have to include even the most dramatic events of your life to have a good story. Practice self-care, and only approach the memories you're ready to take on in the writing process.

Finding your voice.

∞ Before getting started, try speaking your story verbally and recording it. Do your best to speak naturally, as you would if you were telling your story to a trusted friend. Take note of the words you use most often, your cadence, and how you structure your sentences. Maybe transcribe it to see how it flows on the page, then revise it to polish the written form. This way, you can start to see how your unique voice will translate into writing your story in your own way.

∞ Write a letter to a friend (you don't have to send it). Writing your story while addressing a trusted person can help you draw on honesty and compassion for your story. Write it as you would write any letter, and your voice will naturally come through in your existing writing style.

∞ Experiment with writing a memory in two different voices. First, write it from the younger you, experiencing the events in real time. Then, write it as the experienced, older you and how you see the events now. This will force you to separate the events from your current understanding of them.

∞ Write a memory/scene and read it aloud. As discussed in this chapter, this will help you hear how your voice is, or is not, coming through in the writing. Now you can revise the writing to reflect more of your unique voice.

16

WRITING A LIFE
Legacy is Your Gift

I used to always say, "I have a terrible memory." I'd listen in awe as other people spun long yarns about their childhood and the amount of detail they recalled would just amaze me. I didn't have access to that level of detail, not even close. I could remember events from my life, certainly, but it was the "scenes" that I couldn't quite get to.

My Uncle Pat is a great example. He is one hell of a storyteller, and he will suck you in with stories that put you there in the moment. Sounds, smells, and descriptions of the look on someone's face always have me squinting my eyes in disgust or rolling with laughter. It's riveting. I never thought I could do that.

Until I stumbled on my *Ink & Asana* method.

Not only had I found out how to make memories more vivid, I had done it in the name of celebration. I didn't set out to remember things that were buried; I set out to remember with more clarity the memories worth keeping.

I think that was the thing that really got me writing, even though I was never a writer before. The celebration. When we think about "writing our story," our nervous system can lock up. We become frozen because it just seems like too much to take on, and we usually go straight for the difficult memories. The nervous system says, "no thanks!" and we walk away. But when you approach your writing in celebration of your best, most precious memories, then the writing comes easier.

In every fiber of my being, I wanted to remember my time with my mom as clearly as I possibly could. Unlocking stories with yoga, then sitting down to celebrate those memories, had the writing just pouring out.

So, why is it that we "lose" stories even when we remember them? It's because memory is fluid, and it's actually a constructive process. We tend to believe that our memories live in our heads like a giant storage box full of videos. But the truth is that our memories are in there, but they are incomplete. When we attempt to recall them, our minds have to reconsolidate them. This is why the memory may be affected by your current state. Whatever is going on in your life now, the biases you've gathered along the way, or simply your stress level, can affect how that story gets reconstructed, and changes it slightly. Or, it is blocked from fully filling in with detail.

If the story hasn't been revisited often in your mind, the connections weaken, and the memory begins to fade around the edges. It is the act of purposefully going in to extract and retrieve memories that pulls them back into focus. By now you know how we can use somatics to access them.

As the "sandwich" generation, we are watching the window closing on our opportunity to capture precious memories and stories. Our parents are aging, and times are shifting. Kids leaving home, and their childhoods behind put us in the position of launching, while trying to preserve those most important years.

THE KEEPER OF THE FLAME

You aren't just a daughter or a mother, you are a steward of history. Your priority may not be just to protect tangible artifacts from the family's time together, but the intangible heritage, ensuring that nothing is forgotten or distorted.

This isn't about being a "great" writer. Or even a writer at all. It's about building a legacy, a framework, that allows the truth and all those precious bits and pieces to emerge.

So how do you create that legacy? By using a map, instead of just focusing on the pen. Meaning, it's about using tools and creating structure, rather than being a "great writer." That's what allows the past and memories to come into focus.

Midlife is full of transitions. Not the least of which involves the realization that you're torpedoing toward retirement and you're not all that sure about what life will be like when that happens. We all feel it. But once you identify your purpose—that thing we were all supposed to find but ended up in a career that paid the bills—retirement starts to take on a whole new meaning. No longer do you think of retirement as an end, it becomes a thrilling beginning. Your work today stops being just about getting to your retirement magic number in the 401K, and starts being a vehicle that supports you while you build your next adventure. Midlife becomes a homecoming to who you truly are, and that informs who you will become.

As the "sandwich" generation, we are watching the window closing on our opportunity to capture precious memories and stories. Our parents are aging, and times are shifting. Kids leaving home, and their childhoods behind put us in the position of launching, while trying to preserve those most important years.   As   our parents age, we are quickly running out of time to gather their true legacy–that intangible archive of anecdotes, jokes, joys, and pains. I don't say that to scare you. It is my deepest wish that you gather all that you can, while you can. For myself, I didn't realize any of this until my mom was gone. And while that book is my most precious treasure, I wish with all that I have and all that I am that I had written it *with* her.

And it's not just your parents. I don't have any children of my own, but I have nieces and nephews. I see their parents' nest emptying, and I see their childhood—a time sacred to them and to me—fading into the background as they set sail into the wilds of their adult lives. Capturing your own wisdom, and all of your stories, and theirs, together with them, would be an amazing way to pay tribute to those years. Just imagine if your daughter could hold your strength in her hands, just when she needs it the most.

If, when you think of all of that, or look at a picture and try to remember all of the details of that day, you feel a tightness in your chest or gut–that's your body telling you what you need to do.

So, how do you get started? First, set the priority to preserve what you can. We work with an attorney to perfect our wills and our estate plan, to ensure our wishes are carried out. But when it comes to the most valuable form of legacy, we leave it to chance. We hope that we will remember our parents. We pray we will remember our children' s childhood.

My 5-Pillar Blueprint, which I blend with my Chakra Somatic Story Mapping system outlined in the next chapter, will help you create your story and your legacy. Using the ancient wisdom of the energy centers of the body, it automatically has us connecting with the body. Once we do that, we can reconstruct, and then align our story.

The 5-Pillar Blueprint (Legacy Structure)

1. **Origins:** The soil and the roots (Early life, sensory memories of home).

2. **Mirroring & Rites of Passage:** The likenesses between ourselves and our closest loved ones. The fires that forged each individual (Transitions, mystery illnesses, triumphs).

3. **Thresholds & Work:** The hands we admire and our own contribution (Careers, passions, the daily "doing").

4. **The Kitchen Table:** Stories, lessons and the vast wisdom passed down over baked cookies, roasted vegetables, and sitting enjoying a meal. The values and the "No's" that shaped the "Yes's..

5. **The Hand-Off:** The wisdom you've gathered for the next generation. Compiled from past generations, extracted from your own history, you've moved past the boxes of photos and letters to handing over a volume of a lifetime.

Begin by framing your story. We all have those scattered memories, but once you start categorizing them and putting them into an outline that makes sense, they begin to come out of the dark. Couple that with your yoga or mindful movement, and they become vivid and expansive–a gift you didn't know you had within you.

Origins:

These stories are the soil and the roots. Go digging in your garden and you will find stories of growing up, home towns, and ways of being. This is where we find out what made Mom strong, or what made her daughter laugh.

Famously, within our family anyway, there is a story about my mother and her strength of will. One day, in Grandma's kitchen, the little-kid version of my mother was chattering away. Driving my Grandma a little mad, Mom just kept talking. Grandma attempted to silence her one more time, and Mom said, "Mumma, I gotta say what I gotta say, or I'm gonna burst!" To which Grandma replied, "Well then, you better burst!"

I can't tell you how much that little anecdote says about those two women. That about sums them up right there. And while there is a chance we would have always remembered it, it became much more of a conversation piece within our family when my mom and I included it as a part of my Grandmother's eulogy. Then Mom included it in her book about our family. Then I added it to my own book about Mom and me. Now it lives here in this book as well.

Putting a precious story like that in writing keeps it real, not just in print, but imprinted on all of our minds and hearts. We'll never forget it.

Mirroring and Rights of Passage:

Here is where you really relate to each other. How is she like you? How are you not like her? Within this pillar you'll write your core values, what makes you tick. And much of that will come from those challenges and trials in life that carved your character. And hers.

This is your *becoming*.

The story about Mom saying she was going to burst certainly became a mirroring story too–for the three of us possessed our own version of the moxie you see in those lines above. But what comes to mind here are all the times my mother helped me— saved me—from others and from myself.

When I was in college, there was a period of time where we were butting heads about my future. I had decided that she just wanted to turn me into another version of her, and I felt pressured to go a way that didn't feel right to me. But I plead my case in a childish and immature way, so there were some tense letters that went back and forth. Being me, and knowing how I am when my temper flares, I probably said more than I felt.

The only reason I even remember that this happened is because I saved a letter from her. Not ever an overly emotive woman, she would rarely tell me how she felt. But in this letter she told me how what I had said had really hurt her, and that she only wanted the best for me. It was beautiful, sad, and smacked me right out of my tantrum. I kept that letter for a very long time–I might actually still have it. And after I initially received it, I never spoke that way to her again.

I'm so very thankful that I didn't. Our relationship was smooth sailing and lovely ever after that, for the next twenty years that I would have with her.

Thresholds & Work:

My writing in this area began with my mother's hands. I often tell a story about the day my mother passed away. I was sitting at the end of a long hallway, at a sunny table, with a bright window next to me. The men in my life were talking: my husband, father, and brother. But I couldn't hear them; couldn't understand the words. I was strangely concerned with my hands.

All I could think was that they didn't look enough like hers. I was terrified that I would forget her hands—those hands that I had watched my whole life. They were beautiful, graceful, but not delicate. They were strong, and showed me how to do work in the world.

So much of who I am and how I work can be linked back to what I observed as a child. She worked methodically, not too fast, not too slow. The work took the time that it took. She also worked constantly. Never one to sit still for long (unless she was creating a list of all the things she would be doing that day), she was in constant motion. Always finding something to do, she was relentlessly productive.

Speaking of mirroring, I'm sitting here writing this on a Saturday afternoon, after working all day on reworking my journal collection, and managing *Ink & Asana*. I stay pretty busy too.

For years I would think of her hands. But it was only after writing a book about us that I realized how clear the memory of them is for me. I found that I would never forget them, and they were as clear as if I were looking at them right now.

When we bring those memories close, we find gleaming gems like that. Unexpected, and oh so precious.

The Kitchen Table:

This one may very well be my favorite. For me, it calls to mind endless mornings, afternoons, and evenings at my grandmother's kitchen table in Key West. My mom, grandma and I and our long talks.

It's also all the time in the kitchen I spent with Mom, learning how to cook. But it was more than that; it was an act of love. Together we prepared meals, but then spent so much time around the table with the guys, laughing and telling stories.

When I started to extract the wisdom of those conversations, what I thought were fleeting conversations I'd never think of again, I found lessons and growth. I found that there was a time when my father and I would chat back and forth over that table about work.

And as we did, my husband Ricky made an observation that touched my heart. He said that my dad looked at me with immense respect when I talked, and that he could tell that Dad thought of me as a peer. That made me extremely proud.

I loved remembering that, and I'll treasure it always.

The Hand-Off:

You may be able to make a list right now of all the lessons you've learned that you'd like to pass on. For you, they may be top of mind. For some of us, we know we have experiences, but we aren't necessarily consciously aware of the nuggets of wisdom we've gleaned from them. It's amazing how much we have to offer, but when you begin to write, you'll find that the frame may change, and how you tell it shifts.

I'm not sure I had a list in mind when I got started. I just knew I wanted to extract and distill those memories and lessons for my niece and nephew. So I just dove in to fully explore my story. As I did so, the all that good stuff just floated to the surface.

WHERE THERE'S A WHY, THERE'S A WILL

For the empty-nesters: first, breathe. You've done an amazing job. They are heading into their future armed with all you have given them. For you, this time comes with an identity shift. And not only that, it can be tough to figure out what your relationship needs to be like, now that they are adults. Legacy writing, while writing to deepen and re-establish your connection with your child, can help.

This time of transition can also come with some house cleaning and organizing, which can be the perfect time to map out how you will archive their childhood. Think of legacy in this context as looking inward at the home you built for them, as much as you look backward at the past.

It's time for a reframe: you're moving from "I'm losing my role as a daily mother" to "I am becoming the Historian of their lives." Here's where you can get started:

- ∞ The specific language of your home (inside jokes, nicknames, the way Saturday mornings sounded).
- ∞ The "No's" you said as a mother that protected their peace, whether they were aware of it or not.
- ∞ The sensory details: the smell of the sun on their hair, the weight of a sleeping toddler, the chaos of the teenage kitchen.
- ∞ The gratitude engine: the most precious parts of their personality and the times they surprised you.

We all have the first tooth photos. This archive is for the unseen parts of your story.

Creating this archive now matters for your future relationship with your children. Presenting them with an archive of their childhood and all of your time together is an act of Identify Validation. It tells them, "I saw you. I remember. Your beginning was founded in love and intention." Creating a written heirloom captures your legacy, and their history. It's a coming of age ritual for you, helping you process the transition through the act of writing.

Externalizing all of your thoughts and feelings at this moment in time, and through these transitional months, puts them outside of your body. There you can see them, reframe them, and give them new purpose.

Love's Time Capsule

Legacy is the art of deciding what gets to be eternal. It is the building of a sanctuary out of the raw timber cut on good days, and bad. We do not write to record trivial what-nots (although those are always fun); we write to create foundation and load-bearing walls of our character. By choosing which stories to keep, you are creating a shelter where your grandchildren can sit by the fire of your wisdom long after the sun has set on your own horizon.

The Somatic Inquiry:

Grandmother's hands were steady as they buttered your bread. Mother's tea was steeped in story. Daugher's laughter tickled every heart. Close your eyes. Imagine the kitchen table where each gathering was warm, even when someone was cranky. One hand on your belly, and one on your heart—forever connected by a long line of loving care.

Put It Into Practice

Try an archival cleanse: move through the physical house, room by room, and extract the stories before the rooms change function. Take a deep breath and ask, "If these walls could speak the wisdom I learned while raising you, what would they say?"

This is your Middle of Always, and as the child of an aging parent and/or the parent of a launching child, you are the bridge. You can't wait for a "slower time" to write. The stories are freshest now, and your somatic practice will ease you through it.

The medium matters. Make it a beautiful book. That's what I did with my book about my mom and me and for now it is just for me. I may publish it in the future, but there is something so sacred about holding our time together in my hands—just us, just for me. This is the very reason I help my clients create heirloom books. It is a treasure beyond imagining.

There, your legacy will live in their hands, and not just in the clouds of time.

17

THE ENERGETIC BLUEPRINT

Map Your Story

The body is a vertical column of energy. If you've ever experienced a powerful Chakra meditation or energy work, you know exactly what I'm talking about. How can the average person tap into these energy centers to write, heal, and move forward in life with clarity, vision, and purpose?

By now you've learned that the body is a living archive. So we know where everything is stored. Tapping into the physical leads to the unlocking of the emotional, and that let's all those memories flow. But memory doesn't work in chronological order.

Think of the last time a memory just popped in your head out of nowhere. That's the nature of mind. Something somatic—a smell, a sound, the breeze on our face—will trigger a powerful memory. It happens all the time, wildly out of order. The most important parts of our story will be discovered in the same way. But how can we target certain areas of the body to prompt ourselves into writing the stories we want to write?

When you sit down to write and feel blocked, or you're feeling career burnout every time you boot up your work laptop, it's often just a clog in one of your energy centers. It's a story that was lived, but it was never placed down outside of the body. You know as well as I do that when you are tense for extended periods of time, those stories live in your shoulders, or your gut.

I realized that Chakras are a way to map specific somatic practice techniques to each focus area, or energy center, of the body. That's how we begin to extract the stories that are stuck there.

When we tap into those energy centers, stories are unlocked, freeing them from the confines of the body. That is when the flow of writing happens, setting us up for an overhaul of the nervous system. Externalize your thoughts, emotions, and stories, and you take their power away. You begin to respond to them, and to life's stresses, differently.

The Somatic Map: Chakras and Your Story

Before we can begin the "How-To" of extraction, we must understand the filing system of the human experience. While many see the body as a mere vessel for the mind, here, we recognize the body as the primary record-keeper. Just as I found that my stories flowed after a yoga practice, so too you will find that moving a story through and out by writing it ensures it doesn't just settle right back into the same spot.

Your history is not just stored in a cloud; it is stored in your bone marrow, your gut, and the quiet spaces between your ribs. To map these stories, I utilize an ancient vertical blueprint known as the Chakra System.

The Anatomy of Frequency

In the simplest terms, chakras are the seven primary energy centers located along the spine. Think of them as "frequency stations" or "narrative hubs." Each center corresponds to a specific physiological area of the body and a specific psychological layer of your life. When we enlist the chakra system for legacy work, we are not looking for mystical light; we are looking for somatic data. We are looking for where a memory has been "anchored" in the body.

The Seven Extraction Points

To navigate the blueprint, we follow the descent from the Crown to the Root:

The Crown Chakra (Origins & Soil): Your connection to the infinite and the ancestral. This is the attic of the soul, where your highest wisdom and earliest "soil" reside. The crown of the head was the first part of your physical being to enter the world. Here we focus on clarity, spirituality, and purpose.

The Third Eye Chakra (Intuition & Wisdom): Located on your forehead, between your eyes, is your internal guide. The place where you record the moments you knew something before it happened. Your vision, and work: how you show up in the world.

The Throat Chakra (Truth & Voice): The bridge between the heart and the world. This is where your reclaimed "No's" and your undeniable "Yes's" are stored. These are your values.

The Heart Chakra (Love, Compassion, & Forgiveness): The center of you. This is the archive of every love that survived and every grief that transformed you. Your burdens are stored here as well as the lessons they gave you.

The Solar Plexus Chakra (Authority & Power): In your upper abdomen, this is your internal engine. This is where the stories of your fire in the belly and your personal agency live.

The Sacral Chakra (Creative Current, Self-Esteem): Here, in your lower belly, is the pulse of your life. This is the record of your pleasure, your fertility (creative and physical), and your rites of passage.

The Root Chakra (Foundation & Legacy): The subfloor at the base of your spine. This is where you record the safety of your soil and the permanence of the anchor you are dropping. In that soil are the women who came before you, your addition to their gifts is what gets left behind.

WHY THE BODY?

I introduce this system because the mind is a master of editing the past to protect the present. The body, however, cannot lie. When you reach for a memory and your throat tightens, or your stomach flutters, that is a Somatic Signal.

By aligning the 5-Pillar Blueprint with these centers, we ensure that the stories you extract are not just "remembered"—they are witnessed by the very cells and tissues that lived them.

The 5-Pillar Blueprint & Chakra Story Mapping

Before you can start to build, you have to understand the structure of the house. We do not simply "remember"—we reconstruct. This blueprint is your framework, and together with the Chakra Mapping just outlined, we now have a method of aligning the weight of your history with the somatic energy of your body. Here are some examples of how we bring them together and map the extraction.

Pillar 1: Origins – The Soil and the Root

∞ **Chakra Alignment:** The Crown (Arrival). This is the baseline of your architecture. Before you can build a future, you must examine the soil in which you were planted. This pillar focuses on early life, sensory memories of home, and the "ancestral laws" that governed your first decade.

∞ **The Somatic Signal:** When you think of your first kitchen, where do you feel the temperature change in your body? Is there a tightening in the forehead or a softening in the spine? I can almost feel the tension in my neck as I look up to watch my mom working.

∞ **The Extraction:** Look for the "Law of the House"—the unspoken rules of survival and safety that became the subfloor of your current identity.

Pillar 2: Rites of Passage – The Fires of Forging

∞ **Chakra Alignment:** The Sacral and Solar Plexus (Creative Current & Authority). Identity is rarely gifted; it is forged. This pillar documents the transitions, the challenges of mystery illnesses, the big "No's"and the triumphs that moved you from a bystander to a warrior.

∞ **The Somatic Signal:** Locate the buzz in the nest—that internal vibration in the gut or solar plexus that signaled a boundary was being crossed or a power was being claimed. My experience with an abuser puts me on guard every time I encounter another narcissist, even in one conversation. The boundaries go up. My gut says, "never again."

∞ **The Extraction:** Map the fires. What was the heat that finally made you undeniably you? Look for the moments where your creative pulse met your personal authority.

Pillar 3: The Work – The Hands and the Contribution

∞ **Chakra Alignment:** The Solar Plexus and Heart (Power & Work). We are not just what we feel; we are what we do. This pillar examines the careers, the daily "doing," and the passions that have occupied your hands. It is the archive of your contribution to the world's collective machinery.

∞ **The Somatic Signal:** Feel the weight in your hands. What is the rhythm of your productivity? Is it a frantic pace or a steady, grounded hum? I find myself rushing, and my heart connects me to my mother's mindful pace.

∞ **The Extraction:** Look for the common mission across your "series of startups." What is your strength, or the contribution that remains constant, regardless of the job title on your business card?

Pillar 4: The Kitchen Table – The Values and the "No's"

∞ **Chakra Alignment:** The Heart and Throat (Connection & Reclaimed Truth). The Kitchen Table is the center of the home—it is where the "Yes's" are negotiated and the "No's" are enforced. This pillar focuses on your internal values, your capacity for forgiveness, and the reclaimed narratives of your voice.

∞ **The Somatic Signal:** Notice the sensation in your throat when you speak your absolute truth. Does it feel like grounding or a bird taking flight? Who in your lineage does it remind you of?

∞ **The Extraction:** Identify the "No" that shaped your greatest "Yes." Start to map the values that acted as the guardrails for your most difficult decisions.

Pillar 5: The Hand-Off – The Wisdom for the Next Generation

∞ **Chakra Alignment:** The Third Eye and Root (Intuition & Legacy). The final pillar is the hand-off. It is the distillation of your architecture into a blueprint for those who follow. This is the big-picture wisdom—the golden nuggets of life you want to ensure are never erased.

∞ **The Somatic Signal:** Attune to the quiet wisdom in the forehead. What is the feeling of permanence? Is it the knowledge that your experience is now safely part of your family's story?

∞ **The Extraction:** Write one heirloom: what is the one lesson you would leave for your son or daughter?

Your story is the heart of who you are. Your voice is the song of your soundtrack. Your writing is the creation of an archive. It is a gift to you, and to those you love.

By focusing on the chakras, and setting the intention to unlock each energy center through yoga, these connections will begin to happen automatically in your writing.

Put It Into Practice

To begin your own extraction, use these prompts to bridge the somatic signal with your writing.

- ☐ **Origins (Root):** Describe the smell of your first childhood home. What was the unspoken "Law of the House" regarding safety or belonging?

- ☐ **Rites of Passage (Sacral/Solar Plexus):** Recall a moment when your body signaled "No" before your mind could find the words. What power did you claim in the fire that forged you?

- ☐ **The Work (Solar Plexus/Heart):** If your career was stripped of its titles, what is the common thread of service or creation that has always been in your hands?

- ☐ **The Kitchen Table (Heart/Throat):** What is the one truth you once swallowed to keep the peace, and how does your body feel now that you are ready to speak it?

- ☐ **The Hand-Off (Third Eye/Crown):** Imagine your daughter is facing her hardest winter. What is the one undeniable truth from your archive you would hand to her as a lantern?

18

SACRED SPACES
A Yoga Teacher's Way

This one is for those who have made yoga their life.

If you're a current or aspiring yoga teacher, you definitely have a **yoga story** to tell. Of course, if you're reading this book and are not, or don't intend to become, a teacher, you'll have one as well but feel free to jump to the next chapter if this is a little too teacher-y for you. One of my favorite pastimes is hearing about a person's discovery of yoga and how it changed their life. There are so many stories of healing, transformation, and positive change out there—and I know you have one too. Maybe you're thinking about attending your first yoga teacher training class, or maybe you've been a teacher for years—wherever you are on that journey, this chapter is for you.

As a teacher and a writer (whether journaling or writing a story or memoir), you live and work in two parallel and sacred spaces: the mat and the blank page. They're both spaces for self-discovery, and not just for you: as you share your experience, your knowledge, and your hope that what yoga has done for you, you'll be able to give to others. Both of these sacred spaces demand presence, honesty, and a straight-up willingness to meet ourselves exactly where we are. You know as well as I do, that the genuine you—the most authentic self you can muster—that's the draw. That's what your students respond to. And not only that, acceptance of who and what you are, and where you are on your path—that, is the key to opening up to sharing wisdom with the world. The same goes for your writing.

A dedicated writing practice isn't separate from a yoga teacher's development; it's an essential tool for it. Writing is the bridge between the internal, feeling sense of yoga and the external, shared expression of it. For the aspiring teacher, this practice will help you uncover your unique voice and teaching philosophy before you ever lead a class. We all start in a place of insecurity with the shakiness of newness about us, but once you find your true voice, you'll be unstoppable. For the current yoga teacher, this practice will be a wealth of inspiration, preventing burnout, keeping your methods fresh, and elevating your classes from simple instruction to deep and meaningful experiences that your students won't soon forget.

THE INWARD JOURNEY

The first step in finding a voice for the aspiring teacher, or any teacher wishing to reconnect with their foundational "why," is to go within. We can get so caught up in which poses and sequences we're going to use to structure our classes, that it can be easy to leave ourselves behind, losing our own deeply personal practice. When I was going through teacher training, I posed this question to my peer group: "How do you remain connected to your own personal practice now that you're teaching?" I didn't ask because I was interested in the hypothetical; I'd started to feel that everything I did in yoga was about teaching, and my self-exploration had slipped into the background.

Svadhyaya in Writing: The Teacher's Journal

I propose that a non-negotiable for a yoga teacher is your journal. Not a diary, and not the yoga sequencing journal you keep at your side always. This one is a vital tool for self-study. This is where you process the raw data from your practice and your teaching. Here, you can work through post-class and preparation notes. What sensations, emotions, or memories arose during practice today? How can you help your students explore the poses you selected? As you moved through each pose, what did you tell yourself as you were adjusting the pose for how your body felt today? What cues would you give someone else? Write about where you encountered challenges, and where you found ease.

Make notes about philosophy, as in, how did a concept like Santosha show up for you today, on the mat or in life? What are you struggling to understand? What do you want to learn more about?

The challenge for every teacher is translating their internal experience and articulating what they feel into clear language that students can relate to. Writing is the practice ground for this skill. I remember, early in teacher training, the feeling of, "What the hell am I going to say… and when?" I thought I wouldn't be able to come up with my own way—that I might just be a poor copy of my teacher (if I was lucky!). My teacher had us journal throughout the teacher training courses, and it was a lifeline to finding my voice.

Try this: select one pose, like Warrior II. Practice it—take your time getting into the pose, make adjustments, feel your way.

- ☐ What makes the pose feel better, more expansive? What variations and modifications might you suggest?

- ☐ Immediately, write for 15 minutes, looking for the emotional quality of the pose and the energetic directions, and start to build your library of descriptive, original cues. Include hard cues directly related to the pose, like "press the front knee and back foot away from each other," and soft cues, more about tension in the rest of the body, like "relax the jaw" or "soften the eyebrows."

Your power and what draws students to you in particular is your voice—as in, your **core message** and how you deliver it. Doing a great deal of exploration in your journal will help you find what your core message is. It will probably be a version of one of your teacher's messages at first, and that's perfectly fine. You took classes, their message resonated with you, and you want to carry that forward. Nothing wrong with that. But at some point it will evolve into your take on it, and it will change as you incorporate your own discoveries into it.

A great way to unearth your message is to start by writing your yoga story:

☐ How did you arrive at yoga?

☐ What drew you to it, and what was your experience (good and/or bad) when you arrived?

☐ How did that change over time?

☐ Which teachers affected you the most, and what was it about their teaching that really struck you?

☐ What was the moment yoga really clicked for you?

☐ Describe the circumstances that led to you being called to teach.

☐ What specific problem or suffering do you feel most compelled to alleviate through your teaching?

☐ What do you want your students to remember about your teaching?

ENHANCING YOUR CRAFT

Consider how you might **incorporate writing** into your class preparation and delivery. Move beyond the typical method of planning a sequence as a list of poses, and instead think about thematic scripting and sequencing—treating class planning like writing a short story. Begin with arrival, add action (the warm-up and other flows), and work toward a climax (the peak pose), the falling action (backbends, the cooldown, stretches), and then Savasana as the conclusion, with the closing meditation as the resolution. The arc of a class mirrors the arc of a story.

Weave **themes** into your classes, just as you would with writing your memoir. Select your theme, writing it out as you would an intention: "Today, we will explore how grounding down allows us to find expansion and lift up." Choose poses that support your theme, allowing you to work on that very concept, like Warrior poses or Tree. Write a few cues that specifically link the physicality of the pose back to your intention—this is the golden thread of your class. Insert it into the lengthening of the spine in the opening meditation, mention it when rooting down in Mountain at the top of the class and as you move through some of the poses, and then close with it. This adds reinforcement to a physical asana concept like the example above, or to a philosophical concept that you want to teach.

Dharma Talks: From Personal Journal to Universal Offering

Just as your journal, full of memories, insights, flailing missteps, and spectacular victories, serves as raw material for a memoir, so it does for distilling personal reflections that can then be turned into teaching moments. The process that you go through every day, looking at your experience and learning from it so that you can teach others, makes you a perfect potential memoirist. You already know how to do it; it's just a matter of expanding the practice.

For example, think of a time when you struggled with patience (I know I can think of many!). Is there a universal theme there? Certainly so, since you and I, and everyone else, have that in common. The tension, push and pull, between effort and surrender is something anyone can relate to. So, craft the offering for your next class by creating a concise, two- to three-minute opening that introduces the theme and is supported by your personal story. Add your own insights to it to use as an illustration, bringing the concept to life for your students. Then connect it directly to the practice you're about to guide them through.

We can hesitate to include yogic philosophy and concepts in our teaching for fear of not truly understanding them ourselves, but your study, self-study, and exploration of these topics will ensure you understand what it means to *you*.

Writing and yoga are lifelong teachers, as both are practices, not *performances*. Remember that one: it's big. Teaching is a practice, not a performance—just as you teach others to practice, you engage in yours every day. When you're new, it feels like performance, and you think you have to get every little thing "right." But remember that art is life, and expression is art, no matter what it looks like. You are teaching, *expressing*, in your own way—and your students are drawn to you because of *you*.

There's no "perfect" outcome, only the process of showing up. An integrated writing, yoga, and yoga teaching practice ensures that the teacher always remains a student first: ever reflective, curious, and ready to grow. That is the ultimate antidote to stale teaching and burnout.

Your yoga story may be your memoir, for it is most certainly a story of transformation. Give the world the gift of your story, because not only will it help you, but you'll be sending something out into the world that will help others. The other day, I was telling an acquaintance about writing this book, and I included a short version of how I came to yoga. A week later, she said that she'd tried yoga for the first time, loved it, and intended to create a regular practice—just because I told my story. Wow, that just gives me chills.

Isn't that why we do all of this in the first place? We're spreading the joy that we were given.

Trust in your unique voice; write to find it. You'll develop it in ink and embody it in asana and somatic instruction, and it will be exactly what your students need to hear.

PUT IT INTO PRACTICE

☐ Choose a yogic concept you love but feel intimidated to teach (e.g., The Three Gunas, Brahmacharya). Set a timer for 10 minutes. Write a letter to yourself explaining what this concept means to you in your own life. Don't worry about the Sanskrit definitions and official commentaries. How does it actually feel and function for you? Be radically honest.

☐ Using the insights from your letter, design a mini-sequence that embodies the feeling of that concept. Practice the sequence. Now, craft one single cue for each pose that comes directly from the honest language you used in your writing. This is the seed of your next themed class.

19

THE WISE GUIDE INSIDE
Tuning into Inner Wisdom

Our yoga practice encourages us to listen inward, to the subtle whispers of our body and breath. This act of deep listening is the same pathway to accessing our intuition and authentic voice, both on and off the mat, and especially in our writing. When we approach our experiences, particularly those we wish to write about, with this same open awareness, we begin to uncover deeper self-knowledge.

Yoga is inherently a practice of self-study, or Svadhyaya, one of the Niyamas we explored earlier. It asks us to bear witness to ourselves—our physical sensations, our emotional responses, and the constant churn of our thoughts—without judgment. This consistent self-observation cultivates a deep level of self-awareness.

For example, in a pose like Anjaneyasana (Low Lunge, or Crescent Lunge), your teacher might invite you to notice where you hold tension. Is it in your jaw, your shoulders, or your furrowed brow? By simply noticing, you begin to understand your habitual responses to discomfort. Not that you need to fix them immediately, just acknowledge that they're there.

Similarly, in meditation or even during the stillness of Savasana, we learn to observe our thoughts as they arise and pass, like clouds drifting across the sky. We see the stories our minds create, the worries about the past, and the anxieties about the future. This practice of observation creates a space between you and your thoughts, allowing you to see them for what they are: just thoughts, not necessarily truths.

This skill of detached observation, learned on the mat, directly translates to accessing deeper self-knowledge in writing. When we apply this mindful attention to our memories and experiences, we create the opportunity to see them with fresh eyes, unburdened by old judgments or ingrained narratives. That's when our stories go through the wash.

WRITING FROM A PLACE OF TRUTH AND VULNERABILITY

The power of memoir is in the lessons learned, and how they changed the author. It is the chemical process of taking different elements of a story and turning them into something new. That is what makes it worth reading. As I sat writing letters to my mother and, ultimately, memories of us, I was writing for me. Writing what happened was my priority, and that's what I did, striving for pure documentation. But as I explored the memories, I was experiencing them, taking a fresh look at them, and deciding what to do with them—involuntarily at first, then more and more intentionally because I realized the profound shift in my perspective that was at hand. But it took several revision passes for all of it to truly be laundered. It was in those revisions that I sat back, again and again, as an observer, and read what I had written almost as if it had happened to someone else.

But don't fret if you don't yet know what to make of your experiences. I'm not sure I had any idea until it was all over. I remember a moment, as I sat writing the final letter to my mother. I was done with the challenge, I felt like hell, but I'd come out the other side and survived. I had answers, and was awash in so much gratitude for our time together. I'd made several realizations that changed me forever.

In the letter, I recalled the morning my mother passed away. I was sitting at a table at the end of the hall on the hospice floor of the hospital. I was strangely concerned with my hands. As the dust of the day settled into a new reality, I couldn't stop thinking about them, looking at them, and wishing they looked more like hers. They kind of, sort of did, but not enough. I'd watched her hands my entire life; when I was a child, they taught me how to do work in the world. She always took on every task with care and settled in to the time it took to complete it. Never rushing, her hands were beautiful in their way of completing things—her way. That was the memory. In the aftermath of that day, I was crushed with the ultimate totality, but it was her hands I feared I would forget.

It was writing about that, how I was so concerned with forgetting her hands, that got to what was really going on inside, in so many ways, on so many levels.

As I wrote that last letter, it dawned on me: I never forgot her hands, and in that moment I knew I never would. They were as clear in my mind as if I were looking right at them. I realized right then how very vivid it all was—that my heart had a way of "seeing" that gave me perfect clarity in remembering. The fear I had on the day she left was unfounded. I could see all of it—our every moment together—perfectly. And I knew then, sitting at my computer, that I would never forget any of it.

I felt an overwhelming wave of gratitude for that, and for all of it. For the life we'd had together, and even for my illness—because it had given me, and continues to give me, so much. It had all happened, and I persevered. My trauma is still trauma. My grief is still grief. But I hold it differently now, unexpectedly joyful to have gone through it all.

Mindfully Notice Shifts in Perspective

As you revisit and refine your memories, mindfully start to notice any shifts in how you view the story. Imagine you're now seeing it through someone else's eyes, perhaps the eyes of a compassionate friend:

- ∞ If this were your best friend's story that you were reading, instead of your own, what would you tell them?
- ∞ What kindness would you offer?
- ∞ What advice would you give?

It's in asking and honestly answering these questions that you'll start to find what you'll do with your experience and where it will take you. This process of re-framing and re-interpreting, much like adjusting a pose to find deeper comfort and alignment, is where the true transformative power of memoir lies. It's not about changing what happened, but changing your relationship to it.

BEYOND THE VESSEL

Deep within the noise and hustle-bustle of the world, there is a pulse that never falters—a steady, ancient knowing that remembers who you were before society told you who to be. To tune into this wisdom is to touch the Middle of Always. It is the realization that you are not just a student of your life, but a steward of truth that has been waiting for centuries for your heart to live it, and your hand to write it down.

THE SOMATIC INQUIRY:

Place both hands, stacked, over your solar plexus (just above the belly button). This is the seat of your intuition. It's where the wise guide lives. Ask a simple Yes or No question about your story. Does your body lean forward into it, or contract backward away? Trust the physical response over the mental chatter that tries to rule the roost.

PUT IT INTO PRACTICE

To help you interpret events, determine what to do with them, and explore what you've written to come out the other side, consider these practical steps and prompts.

Scan for Emotional Crud

Just as asanas can release physical tension stored in the body, writing can release emotional residue from past events. Choose a memory, and think about it for a moment, noticing how you hold it in your body. How do the emotions associated with it show up for you?

☐ **Free-writing:** Write about this memory as it comes to you, without a filter. Let all the emotions, thoughts, and sensations associated with it pour onto the page for ten to fifteen minutes. Don't worry about making sense.

☐ **Reflection:** After writing, sit quietly. Where do you feel the emotional residue in your body now? Does it feel different than before you wrote? Write about this physical sensation. What insights, if any, arose from simply getting the memory out?

The Witness Perspective

Pratyahara teaches us to be the observer of our thoughts and senses, detaching from their immediate pull.

- ☐ Re-read a passage you've written about a challenging experience. Now, imagine you're a neutral, compassionate witness observing this scene from a distance.

    - ☐ What judgments or criticisms do you still hold about yourself or others in that moment?

    - ☐ If you were advising the "you" in that memory, what gentle wisdom would you offer?

    - ☐ What universal truth or lesson might be embedded in that specific event, if you removed the personal attachment?

When writing about the anger I felt towards my illness and the frustration of feeling unheard by doctors, I initially wrote very raw, angry passages. Applying a "witness" perspective helped me see that beneath the anger was deep fear and a desire for control. As a neutral observer, I could offer compassion to that terrified version of myself, acknowledging the struggle without dwelling in the bitterness. This allowed me to reframe those passages not as simply "angry," but as a desperate plea for understanding and healing, transforming them into a story of strength and self-advocacy, instead of one about being pissed off.

The Future Self Dialogue

Your yoga practice isn't just about the present moment. You're building a foundation for future well-being. As you move through poses, you can envision the stronger, more peaceful human you will become.

- ☐ Write a letter from your future self (imagine yourself five, ten, or even twenty years from now, having integrated the wisdom of your experiences) to your current self:

    - ☐ What challenges have you overcome and what lessons have you learned?

    - ☐ What encouragement, kindness, and advice would your future, wiser self offer about a current struggle or a past event you're trying to process?

    - ☐ What perspective has time and integration given your future self? How does the future you hold themselves, make decisions, and feel about the past?

By consistently engaging with your writing in these mindful ways, you create a dynamic loop of self-discovery. Each time you put your story through the wash, you'll find new layers, new truths, and, ultimately, a new perspective that empowers you to move forward with greater compassion and clarity.

20

THE EXPANSION
Writing Your Yoga

So far, we have spent time with yoga, rolling around in its power to connect us with our bodies, calm our minds, and cultivate inner peace. Next, we took a look at how writing serves as an excavation tool for discovering the self, getting a smack-in-the-face of perspective, processing experiences in unexpected ways, and articulating our straight-up truth. This chapter continues bringing these two practices together, this time shining light on the ways in which writing can become a powerful ally in your yoga practice. The act of putting pen to paper can deepen your understanding of your physical practice, help you integrate the insights gained on the mat, and provide a unique lens through which to not just view, but really *get*, the philosophy of yoga.

Yoga, in all its forms, is a deeply personal path. Every breath, every pose, every moment of stillness offers an experience unique to you. Yet, subtle shifts and profound insights can often be fleeting, disappearing as quickly as they arise. Remember my Savasana ideas? That happens all the time. Sometimes, it's about the yoga itself. I keep a journal and pen within reach from my mat, just in case inspiration strikes, or a question arises, or I want to make note of something to try, work on, or research. It may even be just a simple observation, as I track my progress. The clarity that yoga provides leaves you ripe for idea generation, so keeping a journal nearby ensures those brilliant sparks will be captured.

INTEGRATE YOGA EXPERIENCES

Reframe your yoga practice as a conversation with your body, mind, and spirit. Sometimes it's a gentle whisper, sometimes a challenging debate, and sometimes it delivers a startling revelation. Just as we use language to process our daily interactions, writing provides a structured way to digest the often non-verbal insights gained on the mat.

This is especially useful when you're learning a new way of practicing yoga. Perhaps you've found a new teacher, whose style is different from what you're used to, but it speaks to you. I'm certified to teach Blissology Yoga, founded by Eoin Finn. It's intelligent yoga that really focuses on finding the way a pose fits your body. When I was learning Eoin's way of stretching, it was completely different from what I was used to. I kept my journal with me always, to log what was happening.

One of the major changes was with my forward folds. In Paschimottanasana (Seated Forward Fold), instead of flopping forward and rounding my spine, I was being taught to press the crown of my head or chest forward, and send my hips back at the same time, while anchoring my heels into the ground. Holy moly, what a difference it was making! First, I gave up on getting my nose down to my shins, which was my previous gauge for "success" in this pose. Instead, I focused on the quality of the stretch, and finding *length*; it was no longer about closing the gap and making a smaller angle with my body, it was about getting *long* in every direction. I kept track of my progress and how it was feeling as I went. Even after I gave up on what I thought was an indication of me being more flexible, I actually found that I could now go deeper into the stretch. The telltale sign that I'd been doing it wrong all along, and overstretching at the top of my hamstrings (i.e., a literal pain in the ass), disappeared. Eureka! I was elated. If I hadn't been exploring along the way by writing down my experience each time I took one of his classes, I might not have been mindful enough to really make the change in how I practiced.

It was in that work that my goals for my yoga practice changed. Instead of working to become "advanced" by getting my body to fit into the deepest expression of a pose, I now was interested in the quality of the pose and how it made me *feel*. Total game changer.

Say one day you complete a particularly challenging online yoga class. Perhaps some of the poses felt intensely difficult, or a deep stretch brought up unexpected emotions (I'll admit it: completely unrelated to the yoga itself, I once burst into tears while trying to hold Utthita Parsvakonasana, Extended Side Angle). In the moment, your focus is on the physical sensation and the breath. *Keep it long and steady…* But afterward, the experience might linger, leaving you with questions or an undefined sense of confusion or release. This is precisely when writing can step in as a processing tool.

- ☐ Immediately after a yoga class, or even a few hours later, freewrite about what you experienced. Don't censor yourself. Focus on:

  - ☐ **Physical sensations:** Where did you feel the pose most intensely? Was there pain or ease? Did you tremble? How did your body respond?

☐ **Emotional responses:** Did any emotions surface during a particular pose or breathwork? Did you feel frustration, peace, sadness, joy?

☐ **Mental chatter:** What thoughts arose? Was your mind racing, quiet, or judgmental?

☐ **Unexpected insights:** Did anything click for you? A realization about your emotion, a habitual pattern, or a subtle message from your body?

By putting these experiences into words, you transform them from initial sensation and emotion into a concrete form. This externalization allows you to look at them more objectively, understand their nuances, and begin the process of integration. You're not just feeling it anymore; you're making sense of it. This act of processing is a quiet form of self-therapy, helping your nervous system integrate the shifts that occur during practice.

This may seem a bit too objective, in a way. You may be like me, and when you practice, you just want to feel and try not to think. But inevitably, you will think and feel, and this exercise is just about jotting that down. There's no need to explore every single nuanced bit of feeling you can come up with; just write what you observe, and what you're inspired to write in the moment.

This process is deep yoga, which allows you to select how you'll work through that pose or sequence the next time. Yoga teachers, this is especially relevant to your work. When you're designing a class, it can be very easy to get caught up in the sequence of the poses: does one flow well into the next, pacing, theme, music, etc. Once you've created the class, do it, and *feel* it. Keep your notebook right next to the mat and jot down your thoughts and analysis as you go.

PROGRESS, CHALLENGES, AND INSIGHTS IN A YOGA PRACTICE

A yoga journal is more than just a place to vent; it's a living record of your journey and evolution. Documenting your practice allows you to track your progress, identify recurring challenges, and capture fleeting insights that might otherwise be forgotten. And always remember to address the elephant in the room. No, not that picture of Ganesh on your wall—your ego.

You may be inspired to journal after every class, or maybe just when you've had a powerful experience. Either way, use it to move your practice forward, make notes of questions you'd like to ask your teacher, and remember adjustments or new poses you'd like to learn more about. This adds a layer of connection to your practice that makes any old Tuesday feel more like a yoga retreat.

Are you noticing increased flexibility in your hamstrings? Greater strength in your core? Are certain poses becoming easier or more accessible? Recording these physical milestones can be incredibly motivating and help you appreciate the tangible results of your dedication. For example, after months of struggling to really find length in Forward Fold, maybe you took that cue to press your chest toward your toes instead of your shins, and voila! Your stretch was enhanced in a way you never experienced before. Writing down the day you finally did that can be a powerful affirmation.

Perhaps every time you practice a certain pose, a wave of self-doubt washes over you. Or maybe your mind consistently races during Savasana. Documenting these recurring challenges allows you to become aware of them, which is the first step toward addressing them. Without this written record, these patterns might remain subconscious, impacting your practice without your full awareness.

Yoga often brings moments of profound clarity: a sudden understanding of a philosophical concept, a connection between a physical sensation and an emotional block, or a realization about yourself. These insights are precious. Writing them down immediately, even if it's just a few bullet points, ensures they're not lost. I remember the class where Pigeon Pose changed forever for me. My teacher, Eoin Finn, teaches it this way: before we drop down into Pigeon, rounding the spine and dropping toward the floor, we start in a high place, hips off the ground. From here, we move the hips backward, going back and then down. Here, we wait until the body lets us in, then we start to move forward, always pushing the hips back. Holy macaroni, did that make a difference. In all the years before that, every time I dropped into Pigeon (especially on the left side), my hip would make a "clunking" sound as it shifted into (and out of) place. That was not a healthy stretch, but I would push through it. This new way changed that forever, and I found myself able to get a higher quality stretch that allowed me to progress deeper into the pose.

Your journal will become a testament to your commitment, a source of encouragement on days when you feel stuck, and a reminder of how far you've come. It will shift your practice from a purely physical activity to a holistic path of introspection. And the lessons learned on the mat will inevitably inform your writing. You may end up using your yoga journal entries in your memoir: I know I did.

DEEPENING UNDERSTANDING

I sat on a small cushion, situated in the middle of my yoga mat, the sun beaming through the window and showering me in its light. I could have closed the blinds a bit, but I wanted to feel that warmth on my face. I felt a part of it, no longer apart from it, as my eyes closed over the tears that rolled down my face.

I was a puddle of realization. I'd just written the last letter to my mother that I intended to include in my book. This was the day it dawned on me that my story had been put through the wash, and my past looked completely different. For years, I had held regret and shame, and even grief, in every fiber of my being, without knowing it. But now, I felt this wave of forgiveness toward myself, and I finally shed the shroud of bullshit shame that I'd carried for way too long.

My tears were of joy, of forgiveness, and for the dawning of a new life. I'd written it all out, compelled to the keyboard. Writing about it all, and about my mom, had shown me the way.

I'd realized long before this that the way in which my mom was part of me now was so much more than when she was alive. The best of her lives on in me, and that coach, advisor, and humbling smack-talker gives me advice all the time. My subconscious has adopted what I know she would tell me in any situation, and the writing of our story unlocked what I knew she would say: "Get over yourself. You've had a life. It's not your fault. Forgive."

Pow. Right between the eyes.

Chronic illness had a way of locking me in. I'm sure it's not unusual, but as a perfectionist, getting sick always felt like failing, or the way I would ultimately fail in life. I didn't blame myself for being sick, but I had a particular kind of shame about it, and I was terrified of what it would mean for my future success—in work, and in everything else. I worried it would make me fail.

It didn't. Quite the opposite. It became fuel. And as I closed my letter to Mom, I understood this completely.

I breathed in those realizations, and I reinforced them on the mat. I flowed intuitively, without a set sequence, moving in ways that I felt I needed. I moved all that I'd carried out of my body in an exorcism of the past, of my interpretation of those events. It was all cleansed, and I was finally free.

☐ Of the yogic concepts and principles outlined in this book, which would you apply to me as I sat there that day? Which had I engaged in? What should I incorporate into my asana practice that I learned through writing about my life?

SUPPORT FOR THE NON-LINEAR PROGRESS OF YOGA

"WHOA!!!" That was all I could think, as I stared at the ground in front of me. My hips were up in the air, knees tucked into my armpits, my core strong. No, I wasn't jumping into a pool in cannonball mode; I'd achieved Crow Pose, and stayed there! I felt like I could hang out in the pose all day! This had never happened before, and I was stunned and thrilled.

I had to document how I did it: the strengthening that got me there, and the techniques and cues that I finally really listened to. I felt powerful and advanced, and my ego was singing at the top of its lungs,: "Yesssss!"

About a year later, as I flowed through a Saturday morning class on my favorite online platform, we arrived at Crow Pose. Admittedly, it hadn't worked its way into many classes I'd taken recently, but I knew my body knew how to fly. I looked down, put my knees on my triceps, and leaned into it. I picked up one foot, and then the other. And then I promptly fell on my face.

What went wrong? Feeling my ego smushed by that failure, I consulted my journal after class, and there they were, the cues that had given me success in the past. In my overconfidence and lack of practice, I'd forgotten them. Oops. I realized I should have looked to a spot in front of me, not down, that I hadn't been doing core strengthening, and that it had also been a long time since I'd attempted the pose.

Sometimes, a single yoga experience can be profoundly transformative. It might be the day you finally mastered a difficult pose, the moment a deep stretch released a surge of emotion, or a humbling realization that you need to get back to basics. Writing about these specific breakthroughs allows you to capture their essence and integrate their lessons more fully.

Return to Center

There is a moment when the practice becomes too expansive for the mat and too deep for the journal. It begins to spill over into the world as a homecoming, and a new way of seeing. To write your yoga is to take the alignment, the breath, and the presence you have cultivated and use them to redraw the boundaries of your life. You are expanding the sanctuary until the whole world fits inside it.

The Somatic Inquiry:

Just before sunrise, find a seat facing where the sun will appear. Place your open journal and a pen in front of you. Become your meditative self, with eyes closed, ready to receive. Breathe. As inspired thoughts arise, open your eyes and write them down. Just as they are, no editing. Close your eyes again and breathe. As the sun rises, watch as the poetic words flow through you to the page.

Put It Into Practice

Take out your **yoga journal**, and take a few minutes to explore, using the prompts below:

- ☐ How does the concept of "sthira-sukham asanam" (steadiness and ease in a pose) translate to your daily life off the mat? How do you find ease in challenging situations, or steadiness amidst chaos?

- ☐ What actions have you taken in your yoga practice or your life that have led to positive or negative outcomes? What have you learned from these?

- ☐ What is your unique purpose or path, and how does your yoga and writing practice help you align with it? If you don't yet know your unique purpose or path (because you do have one!), that's okay—how can you use your yoga and writing practice to determine what it is?

- ☐ Choose a specific yoga class, pose, or meditation session that felt like a turning point for you.

  - ☐ What led up to this experience?

  - ☐ What happened during it, moment by moment?

  - ☐ How did you feel afterward?

□ How did this experience change your understanding of yourself or your practice?

□ Use a metaphorical approach to describe a challenging pose or a difficult period in your practice. For instance, if your experience in a long hold in Warrior
III felt like navigating a storm, describe the "wind"
(thoughts), the "rain" (emotions), and how you found
"shelter" (steadiness, breath). This creative approach
can unlock deeper insights and personal meaning.

□ Imagine your body, or a specific part of it, can speak.
Write a dialogue between your conscious self and your
body about a persistent ache, a joyful release, or a new
capability gained through yoga. What is your body
trying to tell you? What do you need to acknowledge
or understand?

PART III

THE PRACTICE

Ink & Asana in the Real World

21

THE SETUP
Designing Your Integrated Practice

We've taken a wild ride, up into the bright sunlight and breezes of yoga's ancient wisdom and down into the valley forest and deep pools of mindful writing. You've seen how both practices nurture presence, self-awareness, and the ability to truly listen to yourself. Now, it's time to weave them together into a seamless, sustainable practice that speaks directly to your unique needs and desires.

The beauty of an integrated practice lies in its flexibility and personalization. The way you do this will be yours alone. There's no one-size-fits-all schedule, just as there's no single "right" way to practice yoga or write. The key is to create a rhythm that feels supportive and sustainable, allowing both disciplines to feed and enhance each other.

Before you even pick up a pen or roll out your mat, take a moment to listen to your body and your life. What does your current schedule look like? When do you feel most energized? When do you crave stillness or introspection? Are you a morning person or a night owl, or do you thrive in the quiet of the afternoon? What are you spending time on now that doesn't serve you or your intentions?

Start to identify pockets of time in your schedule that you can dedicate to either writing, yoga, or both. I'm a morning and evening writer, but I prefer (and have time for) yoga in the evening—except on the weekend, when I'm all about morning yoga with a writing session directly after. I make notes and journal over morning tea. I've given up the news and social media during this time of the day, and it's been worth every minute. After work in the evening, I go right to the mat; it's the perfect disconnection and reset between my work life and my personal space in the day. After yoga, we have dinner and watch a good show or two. Then I write for about an hour or so, before it's time to start my decompression process and get ready for sleep.

What time of day do you feel most creative? When does your body feel most like moving? When is your mind the most clear? Can you combine current activities (like how I still take time with my morning tea, but work on writing instead of consuming media)?

Once you make a plan, you guessed it, write it down. Put it in your calendar in blocks, and set reminders. Write it in your journal and refer to it daily. When you're starting a new habit, you'll need to turn on the Tapas a bit, and be disciplined about it. Eventually, it will be so natural you won't have to think about it, but at first, you may need to work on it. Be patient, and the practice will soon become second nature. You'll crave it, always ready to write, always ready to do some yoga.

So, let's pause for an important message from your guide. Let's take a moment to talk about **patience**. For I, my dear friend, am NOT a patient person. Oh, far, far from it. If there is a patience spectrum, I don't think I'm on it. I'm not sure I can begin to describe to you how fast I work on projects like this book. I carve out every spare minute I can find and I virtually pour it out of myself. Why, you ask? Because I have the patience of a monkey who wants that banana in your hand. GIMME! I want a finished book, and I want it now.

I'm making this grand admission to you, in written form, in an effort to get myself to knock it off. I mean, the intensity is a good thing: I get work done like you wouldn't believe. But I also feel at times like a pressure cooker—and I need to open the valve.

It takes the time that it takes.

Say it with me. "It takes the time that it takes." I promise to remember that, if you'll do the same. If, at this point, having read all the previous chapters about how wonderful your integrated yoga and writing practice is going to be, you're feeling just plain overwhelmed, don't worry. It will take the time that it will take for you to work in all of the little tidbits that you selected to try. All those prompts, creative sparks, methods and exercises—you'll get to them.

Select a few to begin with, and just get started. The rest will come in time.

Together, we shall breathe… and begin again.

To this day, more than ten years after my mother's passing, I still take inspiration from her hands. They were beautiful, graceful, but not delicate. She worked constantly, on all kinds of projects—from writing, to housework, to gardening, to research, to home repairs, to designing games and itineraries for family trips, to setting up a sanctuary and caring for me when I was sick. And they took their time, those hands. Each task was done without rushing, but with enough dedication and moxie to get it through to satisfactory completion. Those hands taught me to do work in the world. But I have to remind myself to slow down, because she was far more patient than I.

I vow to do as she did. When I find myself rushing to get to a first draft, or spending too much time on a project, I'll pause. I'll take a break, breathe deeply, do a little yoga, and remember that it takes the time that it takes.

I'll be back in a little while.

That's better. Let's continue…

WEAVING THE PRACTICES TOGETHER

The true magic happens when yoga and writing become intertwined, each serving as a gateway to the other. Here are a few practical ways in which you might combine them. In Chapter 22, I'll give you a system for taking your *Ink & Asana* practice into daily life, but we'll start with an overview, so you can start to envision how you can make the combined practices work for you.

Morning

Many find the morning to be an ideal time to integrate these practices, as it allows you to set a calm, intentional tone for the day.

Option 1: Yoga first, then write.

- ∞ **Yoga (15-30 minutes):** How you practice is a personal choice that depends on where you are in your yoga journey, and how you prefer to flow. Depending on the day, I like to vary whether I just click to start an online class with my favorite teacher, go through sequences on my own, or of course attend a live class here and there. Whatever you choose, keep it simple and achievable, and make it a practice that eases you into your day.
    - ∞ A sample sequence: Three Sun Salutation A's, followed by Cat–Cow, Child's Pose, and some gentle front-body stretches like Cobra or Upward Dog. Follow that with a Warrior flow: step into Warrior I, stretch into Warrior II, open up into Reverse Warrior, and then pull back to Downward Dog. Repeat on the oth-

er side, then do some seated forward folds, like Paschimottanasana or Baddha Konasana, to close. And, of course, Savasana, before ending with some Pranayama in a seated position. If you're newer to yoga, don't worry about doing a sequence on your own—click into an online class and let the teacher guide you.

∞ **Writing (10-20 minutes):** Transition directly from your mat to your journal or writing space. With your mind clear and your body open, engage in morning pages, free-writing, or a gratitude practice. Or, work on whatever writing project you have going. The stillness and presence cultivated in yoga often make it easier to access your inner thoughts and drop your feelings onto the page. You might find that themes or insights from your yoga practice naturally emerge in your writing.

Option 2: Write first, then yoga.

∞ **Writing (10-20 minutes):** Begin by emptying your mind onto the page. I don't know about you, but I sometimes wake up early with ideas running around like proverbial headless chickens. So, I get in front of my keyboard and just go. This could be a brain dump, a reflection on a dream, or processing any anxieties before the day begins. This act of externalization can create mental space.

∞ **Yoga (15-30 minutes):** Use your yoga practice to embody the clarity you've gained or to release any lingering emotions. Since you've laid your thoughts down in the writing process, you can leave them behind and just feel. The movement and breath can help integrate your insights and prepare you physically and mentally for the day ahead.

Mid-Day

If mornings are too hectic, or you find yourself needing a break from work or daily demands, a mid-day integration can be incredibly powerful:

- ∞ **Yoga (5-10 minutes):** A few seated stretches at your desk, a quick Cat-Cow on the floor, some deep side stretches, or a short walk with mindful breathing can shift your state of mind.

- ∞ **Writing (5-10 minutes):** Use this time to check in. How are you feeling? What thoughts are circulating? A quick stream-of-consciousness entry or a bulleted list of reflections can help you process the first half of your day and re-center before continuing.

- ∞ **Brainstorming:** If you're anything like me, you might have ideas throughout the day when you're working on a project like a book. So, use a notes app, or keep a journal nearby, so that you can make quick notes about any brilliant ideas that pop up during your workday.

Evening

The end of the day is a perfect time to process experiences, release tension, and prepare for restful sleep:

- ∞ **Writing (15-30 minutes):** Journal about your day. What went well? What challenged you? What insights did you gain? This allows you to download and digest the day's events, preventing them from swirling in your mind as you try to sleep.

- ∞ **Yoga (15-30 minutes):** Follow with a calming, Restorative Yoga practice. Yin Yoga, gentle stretches, or a long Savasana can help you release physical tension and quiet the nervous system. The themes you explored in your writing might find a deeper release or integration in your body through these poses.

For my evenings, yoga after work resets me and just clears the day away. I connect and decompress further by spending time with my love. So, by the time I get to writing, I feel clear and ready. Experiment with different schedules, and find what works for you.

Dedicate a longer session once or twice a week—perhaps on a weekend—to a more expansive practice.

- ∞ **Yoga (60-90 minutes):** This could be a longer flow, a dedicated Yin or Vinyasa practice, or an online class that allows for deeper exploration of poses and breathwork.

- ∞ **Writing (30-60 minutes, or more if you are inspired):** Use this extended time for more in-depth writing. This might be a significant free-writing session, working on a memoir chapter, or exploring a complex emotional theme that arose during your yoga practice. This extended session allows for profound integration and breakthrough.

START SMALL, BE CONSISTENT

The biggest mistake people make when starting a new routine is trying to do too much, too soon. Begin with what feels manageable. Even five minutes of mindful breathing and five minutes of journaling each day is a powerful start. Consistency beats intensity every time when it comes to a new habit. It's better to do a little bit consistently than to attempt an hour-long practice once a month. When I started yoga, it was daily, but it was gentle—and over time, the intensity increased. When I started writing, it was a little bit at a time, primarily because the emotions and trauma it raised were tough to handle in large quantities.

Listen to yourself, and remember, it'll take the time that it takes. As you become more comfortable, you can gradually increase the duration or frequency. This is your practice, designed by you, for you.

SETTING INTENTIONS

A goal is one thing, and an intention is quite another. It's a guiding principle, a quality you wish to incorporate, or a particular focus you bring to your practice. Setting intentions transforms a series of exercises into a meaningful journey of self-discovery.

Why set intentions? Intentions create focus, helping you stay present and preventing your mind from wandering. They infuse your practice with purpose, making it more than just a task. Intentions set the tone, guiding your choices on the mat and in life, as well as your writing. They're a great way to bridge the physical, mental, and emotional parts of you.

In yoga, an intention is often called a Sankalpa. Your heartfelt desire or resolve, it's typically stated in the present tense, as if it's already true, which I love. How beautiful is that? It's a done deal. Strive for quality in your intention setting. Instead of "I want to be more flexible," try "I am open and free." Instead of "I want to relieve stress," try "I am calm and at peace." Focus on somatic sensations: "As the breath comes in, my side ribs expand," or "I embody strength and power in this pose." And as you practice, intentions can be used to connect to your daily life: "May this practice help me develop patience that I carry into my day," or "I move with gratitude," or "I enjoy every single breath."

State your intention silently at the beginning of your yoga practice, perhaps while in a comfortable seated position or during the first few breaths. Let it permeate your being as you move through your poses. Find a spot to repeat it during the practice, and again at the end. As you sit cross-legged, or in half-lotus to close your practice, breathe into your intention, and exhale barriers or negative self-talk.

Your writing intentions can be both broad and specific, guiding what you choose to write about and how you approach the act of writing itself: "I will write my truth, approaching with courage," or, "I will allow myself to recognize and appreciate my past experiences, and use them to grow." Setting intentions like these take the power away from your past, or your memories, and puts it squarely in your lap. You are in charge, and you are intentionally approaching the work with a peaceful mind.

Before you begin a writing session, take a moment to pause. Close your eyes, take a few deep breaths, and ask yourself: "What do I need from this writing time today?" or "What quality do I wish to bring to my words?" Let the answer arise, and then begin to write with that intention in mind.

The beauty of integrating your practices is that your intentions can span both. For example:

∞ Yoga intention: "I am releasing tension in my body."

∞ Writing intention: "I am releasing pent-up thoughts and emotions onto the page."

Notice how the physical release in yoga can inform the emotional release in writing, and vice versa. To me, it seems like yoga jogs the tension and emotions loose so that I can then see them more clearly. Then I release them into the wilds of my journal or the structured scenes of a memoir.

FINDING TIME

When changing our behavior, starting a new hobby, or beginning a meaningful practice like writing and yoga, it can feel like a lot. *How will I find the time?* I used to wonder that too.

Priorities matter. When I was at my sickest and just needed my time in yoga to feel some form of relief, it was a no-brainer: I practiced for an hour or two every single day. As I began to feel better, I fell back into daily practice—and it wasn't a choice, it was just what I was used to doing. Setting a habit takes time. You have to choose an activity every day, for about a month or so, and after that, it'll just happen. If a day came and I didn't step on the mat, it felt strange.

I stumbled more when it came to writing. Until, again in crisis, I turned to the keyboard to write to my mother, and then write our memories. I had stops and starts, I couldn't think what to write, and I didn't know where to begin. I just kept deciding to do it. Until one day, it was no longer a decision, and I just showed up at my keyboard every time I had a spare minute.

Make the commitment first, and over time, you won't have to try. That's not to say there won't be days when it can be challenging and maybe not as productive as you'd like, but showing up to do the work is the important part.

One of the primary ways I found time was to quit social media, at least for the most part. I stopped the endless scrolling. I was appalled at how much time I found by doing that, which I could now repurpose to more meaningful activities.

What if these activities were in your daily schedule: 60 minutes of yoga, 45 minutes of writing, 30 minutes of reading, 15 minutes of meditation? That's 2.5 hours, which is 15.6% of a 16-hour day. That may seem like a lot. But think of your day. In the morning over tea or coffee, how much time do you spend staring at your phone—30 minutes? At lunch, same question—15 minutes? Throughout the day—another 30 minutes? At the end of the day—another 30? In the evening, how much time do you spend watching shows or spending more time on another device? Add it all up… you might be surprised.

Assess and set priorities. How much time do you really need scrolling? Can you check in on friends and family in less time? How much time do you need watching your favorite shows? Some decompression time is absolutely a good thing, sure, but do the math, then carve out time for your beloved and sacred practices. You're worth it.

BEYOND COMMITMENT

While you can make a commitment to a daily yoga and writing practice, it's important to make it easy for yourself to fulfill the promise you make to Future You. For yoga, an online platform makes daily practice a cinch, and it's also affordable. Don't discount the power of community in a live class, however; you may still want to incorporate that into your rotation. When you use an online platform, the yoga will be guided—select a video or a class and go. All you have to do is show up on the mat.

The writing comes from within, and while there are videos and prompts that inspire, sitting down with the intent to write your stories can be intimidating. Give yourself the space to learn and grow, especially if you're new to writing or find yourself blocked. Start small—you may have memories that are tough to face at first, so work small, then expand your writing time each day. For timed exercises, just write—it doesn't matter what it is, let your pen or your fingers fly. Write out everything that comes to mind. Don't cross anything out, don't correct spelling or other errors. This exercise is about giving up control. If you hit on something that's right in the middle of your trauma, your grief, your fear, dive straight into it and write it out. Expel it. Writing is a practice and, like yoga, the more you do it, the more flexible and agile you become and the less you have to decide to do it; it becomes something you crave and is automatic.

Take out the trash. As you write, you'll be delighted to see the volume of material that you're capable of producing, but at some point you have to ask, is that part of the story worth telling? Does it serve the themes you're trying to stick to? Does it move your story forward? Inevitably, some of what you write will be tossed out—sometimes even your favorite stories. That's if you are writing a memoir for public consumption. If it's for you, or your family, keep whatever you want.

The word "practice" appears about a bazillion times in this book, but let's take just a second to really think about the word, and why we use it to describe our *Ink & Asana* work. We are all in practice. Practice doesn't make perfect; practice makes *progress*. The challenge is only to keep at it.

And finally, remember that what matters most is your *expression*. Your life is art. Your yoga is art. Your writing is art. It is the doing that is the accomplishment. Your passion, your commitment, your offerings will inform what it looks like and who it speaks to, but it's the art that is *you* that will make others sit up and take notice.

The Soul's Loom

To build this practice is to erect a cathedral in the center of your kitchen. It is the radical act of claiming your square of earth and a sliver of time and declaring them sacred. When you set the stage for your Ink & Asana, you are telling the universe that your soul's work is worth the silence. You are creating a way to hold time, where the clock stops and legacy begins.

The Somatic Inquiry:

Walk through your home in your mind. Where does the air feel the most still? When you imagine yourself sitting in that spot to write, does your breath become deeper or more shallow? Just as the body remembers more than the mind, it also knows where your sanctuary is before the mind does.

22

COMPASSIONATE ACTION
From Within to the World

The world we live in is rife with opportunity to become overwhelmed and frustrated. More than ever, we're fractured, divided, and struggling to see each other's point of view. The political world has spun out of control, and it can make us feel helpless and lost. Our *Ink & Asana* tools can help us channel that energy into something positive. Don't berate yourself for your negative feelings and pent-up aggravation—turn it into something else. Use it to light a fire within.

Writing and yoga can create immense inner change, but what we do next matters. The world needs your insights, your wisdom, and your energy. So send it out. Take that positive change that you've created within yourself and share it, bringing yourself more accomplishment and satisfaction at the same time. Helping others is a balm for the soul.

This chapter is about translating your inner work into outer action. We'll look at how you can clarify your unique contribution, find your voice, and step into the role of an embodied activist. Your goal may not be to become an "activist" per se; instead of engaging in large-scale change, maybe you're just interested in simply infusing your daily life with conscious, compassionate action. Either way, it's a contribution to a kinder world.

FINDING YOUR PURPOSE: CLARIFYING YOUR CONTRIBUTION

Before you can effectively take action in the world, it's important to understand why you want to act and what truly gets you fired up to do something. Your purpose isn't something you find outside yourself; it emerges from the intersection of your deepest values, your unique talents, and the issues that ignite your passion. Your integrated practice has already begun to light your way.

Your writing practice, a mirror reflecting your headspace, is an invaluable tool for clarifying your purpose. What consistently appears on the page when you free-write? What themes resurface in your journal entries? These recurring thoughts, concerns, and desires are signs pointing to your passions and core values.

- ☐ For 10–15 minutes, write without stopping about the local, societal, political, or global issues that really bother you. What injustices make your blood boil? What problems keep you up at night? What rights are being threatened by big orange monsters? Don't censor yourself. Let the anger, frustration, or sadness pour onto the page. This isn't about solutions yet, but about identifying what sticks in your craw.

- ☐ Imagine a world where all the issues you identified in the previous prompt are resolved. What does it look like? What does it feel like? How are people interacting? Describe it in vivid detail. This exercise helps clarify your vision for a better future, which is often a direct reflection of your purpose.

- ☐ Write a letter to yourself from 50 years in the future. This is your legacy letter. What do you want to be remembered for? What impact did you make? What contributions did you offer to your community or the world? This helps distill your long-term aspirations and the kind of legacy you wish to leave. It's the foundation for creating a map to get there.

☐ Make a list of all the activities you engage in regularly. Next to each, write whether it energizes you or drains you. Maybe use an up arrow or "+" sign for those that energize you, and a down arrow or "-" sign for those that drain you. Pay particular attention to activities that give you a sense of flow or deep satisfaction. These are often aligned with your natural talents and passions.

By consistently working with these prompts, you'll start to see patterns emerge, revealing the causes and concerns that genuinely resonate with your spirit. You may have known what they were before ever entering those exercises, but hopefully they helped you give some clarity to all the issues that are important to you.

Your yoga practice has taught you presence and self-awareness. Your writing has helped you articulate your unique view of the world. Now, extend that awareness outward. The ability to listen to your body's subtle cues can be mirrored in your ability to tune into the subtle (and not-so-subtle) needs of the world around you.

Think about the lessons you've learned on your mat and in your writing: power in challenging poses, compassion for insecurity, the release of tension, the clarity gained from confronting difficult stuff. How can these internal shifts inform your way of dealing with, or confronting external issues?

Perhaps your personal journey with chronic illness has ignited a passion for healthcare advocacy. Or maybe the tools and life skills you've acquired through your experience and their ability to help others do the same has inspired you to write a book (wink). Maybe processing grief has led you to support others facing loss. Your unique experiences aren't just for your own growth; they're often your fuel for action.

Purpose is a concept and a feeling, a visceral sense of attunement that you can zero in on and recognize in your body. Your yoga practice, with its emphasis on embodiment, helps you connect with this feeling.

THE EMBODIED ACTIVIST: TAKING ACTION

With a clearer sense of purpose, you're now ready to move beyond feeling powerless and into taking action. This doesn't necessarily mean joining large-scale protests (though it certainly can!). It means living your purpose through conscious choices and consistent steps, large and small. An embodied activist is someone who acts from a place of inner alignment, rather than reactive exhaustion.

The world's problems can feel overwhelming, leading to a sense of helplessness. Your integrated practice counters this by cultivating presence and personal agency. When you feel grounded and clear, you're better equipped to identify manageable actions rather than succumbing to paralysis. There have been times, over the last decade or so, when I felt frozen by the overwhelm, unsure where to start—and maybe you can relate.

We start with ourselves, then we take one small step. Your writing may be the way that you take action. Instead of focusing on the enormity of a problem or issue, start by finding one problem or organization you feel you can get behind. Or start a petition. Or, even smaller, just start sharing meaningful (and fact-checked!) content that gets people thinking. Be a force for facts—there is so much misinformation that even the best of us can get caught in the trend. Information wormholes are real, and whatever bubble you're in makes you think that everything you see is real. It's not. Everyone is an influencer and interested in your click more than anything else—it's how they make money. Proceed with caution. Research with care.

Recognize that whatever you do, no matter how small the act, it create ripples. Kindness matters, and how we treat each other reverberates through society. Send energy into the world that can inspire others to drive positive change.

Activism comes in many forms, and your purpose will guide you toward how to express yourself. Here are some ways in which you may wish to engage:

∞ **Direct advocacy:** Writing letters to elected officials, signing petitions, making phone calls, attending town halls or peaceful protests.

∞ **Community engagement:** Volunteering your time, joining local advocacy groups, participating in community cleanups, supporting local businesses aligned with your values.

∞ **Conscious consumption:** Making ethical purchasing choices, reducing your environmental footprint, supporting fair trade.

∞ **Personal influence:** Engaging in respectful dialogue, educating yourself and others, leading by example in your daily interactions.

∞ **Creative expression:** Using your writing, art, or other creative talents to raise awareness, inspire empathy, or articulate solutions.

Your integrated practice provides a powerful toolkit for effective, sustainable activism. Lean into it:

∞ **Take a moment of Pranayama for grounding.** Before entering a potentially stressful situation (a difficult meeting, a challenging conversation, a protest), take a few minutes for Ujjayi Breath or Box Breathing. This calms your nervous system, allowing you to respond from a place of presence rather than reactivity.

∞ **Take an embodied stance.** In moments of intensity, consciously root your feet, lengthen your spine, and soften your jaw. This physical grounding can help you maintain emotional equilibrium and project strength and clarity.

∞ **Practice mindful listening.** Just as you listen to your body in a pose, practice mindful listening when engaging with others, especially those with differing viewpoints. Listen not just to their words but to their emotions and underlying concerns.

You may choose to craft a letter to an elected official, or write a blog entry or an op-ed. If so, take some time to prepare, and consider your message:

∞ **Clarify your message.** Before you write, get clear on the core message you want to convey. What is the specific issue you're addressing? What is your proposed solution or call to action? Use free-writing or journaling to distill your thoughts and emotions around the topic.

- ∞ **Know your audience.** Who are you writing to? A letter t o an elected official requires a different tone and structure than an op-ed for a general audience. Research their positions, their concerns, and the best way to reach them effectively.

- ∞ **Craft with intention:** Every word matters. Use your writing practice to choose language that's clear, concise, and impactful. Avoid jargon and emotional appeals that might alienate your reader. Focus on presenting facts, personal stories (used thoughtfully), and a compelling argument.

- ∞ **Use revision as empowerment.** Your inner critic might tell you that your first draft isn't good enough. Remember the lessons of putting your story through the wash. Embrace revision as an opportunity to strengthen your message, refine your arguments, and ensure your voice is heard.

- ∞ **Share your embodied voice.** When you write from a place of inner clarity and purpose, your words carry a different weight. They're authentic, resonant, and more likely to inspire action in others.

Activism is a marathon, not a sprint. Creating a sustainable way for you to remain engaged requires taking good care of yourself. Watch for burnout. If you're feeling overly fatigued, or find yourself getting irritable or pessimistic, prioritize rest and self-care. Use your integrated *Ink & Asana* practice; it's not just a set of tools for self-discovery, but it informs our activism and is a way to replenish our energy. There is so much to be done that it can be too much to take in, so learn to say no to commitments that overextend what you're willing to give.

And most importantly, don't lose your joy. Connect with other activists, and dive face first into community, for it is those other humans who make it worthwhile. Find those other people who understand not only what you want to do to make positive change not only in your own life but in the world. Take care of you, and remember to tap into that place inside that's always happy, always joyous, for no reason at all. And one day, we will move the world toward a better way of being: kinder, more equitable, safer, more what we are working for.

23

LIVING INK & ASANA
Sowing the S.E.E.D.S. of Change

It's Ink-ish. It's Asana-eque. It's do-able, and it's time to get started. Here's a system to help you make *Ink & Asana* a reality.

THE INK & ASANA S.E.E.D.S. SYSTEM

Welcome, my friend, to a journey of finding self, enjoying your perfect imperfections, and marveling at your creative blossoming. It's time to tap into that pull you feel to connect more deeply with your body, to unlock the stories held within, and to express them authentically in your writing. What follows is your roadmap.

This is the *Ink & Asana* S.E.E.D.S. system—a gentle, yet powerful framework designed to integrate mindful movement and reflective writing into your daily life.

S–Somatics

Attunement to the internal experience of the body and the asana practice.

E–Embodiment

Consciously integrating and experiencing each moment and movement.

E–Exploration

Writing with a pure heart and dedication to personal truth.

D–Deepening

Unearthing change, gaining perspective from your writing.

S–Surrendering

Releasing the need for perfection and trusting the process.

This system, at its core, is about cultivating a profound mind–body connection. It recognizes that our bodies hold stories, emotions, and wisdom, and that by listening to them, we can access a richer well of material for our writing. Whether you're a seasoned yogi and writer or just beginning to step your toe on the mat or to put pen to paper, the *Ink & Asana* S.E.E.D.S. system offers a holistic approach to creativity and self-expression.

WHY S.E.E.D.S.?

In our crazy world, full of self-help tips and tricks, life hacks, and amazing promises of transformation, it's easy to say we're going to put something new into practice, but making it happen can be difficult. We can live primarily from the neck up, disconnected from the subtle wisdom of our physical selves, from the stories our bodies are waiting to tell. The *Ink & Asana* S.E.E.D.S. system gives you a daily structure and invites you to slow down, to feel, and to listen.

S.E.E.D.S. IN DAILY LIFE

The beauty of the S.E.E.D.S. system lies in its adaptability. It doesn't require hours of dedicated time;   instead, it encourages consistent, mindful engagement. Here's how you can begin to weave it into your everyday.

Option 1: Let the River Run (45-120 minutes)

This option is perfect for those who prefer guided yoga practices, on days when some time is available but it's not too plentiful. Customize the components and how much time you'd like to spend on each, depending on your schedule and what you feel you need that day.

∞ **S–Somatics (5-10 minutes):** Begin by closing your eyes and bringing awareness to your body. Notice any tension, tingling, or warmth without judgment. *Before pressing play on your chosen online yoga class, take a moment to sense into your body. What does it feel like right now? Where are you holding tension? What sensations are present?* This will help you select the type of yoga class you need that day, and how you will approach it.

∞ **E–Embody (20-45 minutes):** Engage in your online yoga class. As you move, consciously feel each pose. Rather than just going through the motions, focus on the stretch, the breath, and the sensations in your body. In Savasana, simply be open to receiving insights, without trying to generate them.

∞ **E–Explore (10-50 minutes):** After your practice, sit down with your journal or memoir project. Write about the yoga practice, or write whatever ideas you're having in the moment. Let the body-mind connection be your inspiration for writing.

∞ **D–Deepen (10-15 minutes):** Review what you've written. Can you identify a single insight, an image, or a powerful idea that emerged? Highlight it, circle it, or rewrite it on a fresh page. This is your "nugget of truth" for the day. If you're working on a book, use the longer amount of time to write.

∞ **S–Surrender (1 minute):** Close your journal, shut your laptop or tablet, put your pen down. Trust that the work is complete for now. Release the need for perfection, and breathe. Just as we do in Savasana, where the body begins to integrate what it's learned, so too does our story as we leave it for the day.

Option 2: Showing Up (15-35 minutes)

Ideal for busy days when time is short, but the desire for connection remains. We don't always have as much time as we'd like to spend on our integrated practice, but showing up consistently matters. As you carve out what time you can, work your practice in:

∞ **S–Somatic scan: (1-2 minutes):** Close your eyes and slowly bring awareness to different parts of your body, noticing any areas of tension, gripping, tingling, or warmth.

- ∞ **E—Embody (10-20 minutes):** Follow a mini yoga class video or do some gentle, intuitive movement. This could be a few Sun Salutations, gentle stretches, or whatever poses your body needs.

- ∞ **E—Explore (3-10 minutes):** Journal or jot down ideas for your book.

- ∞ **D—Deepen (1-2 minutes):** Re-read your writing and find the most impactful phrase, image, or idea.

- ∞ **S—Surrender (30 seconds):** Close your journal or laptop, and let it go until next time.

Option 3: Balance (45-180 minutes)

For when you have plenty of time, perhaps on the weekend when you can deep dive into yoga and writing:

- ∞ **S—Somatics (5-10 minutes):** Begin by closing your eyes and bringing awareness to your body. Notice any tension, tingling, or warmth without judgment. *Before pressing play on your chosen online yoga class, take a moment to sense into your body. What does it feel like right now? Where are you holding tension? What sensations are present?* This will help you select the type of yoga class you need that day, and how you will approach it.

- ∞ **E—Embody (20-90 minutes):** Engage in your online yoga class. As you move, consciously feel each pose. Rather than just going through the motions, focus on the stretch, the breath, and the sensations in your body. In Savasana, simply be open to receiving insights, without trying to generate them.

∞ **E–Explore (10-60 minutes):** After your practice, sit down with your journal or memoir project. Write about the yoga practice, or write whatever ideas you're having in the moment. Let the body–mind connection be your inspiration for writing.

∞ **D–Deepen (10-15 minutes):** Review what you've written. Can you identify a single insight, an image, or a powerful idea that emerged? Highlight it, circle it, or rewrite it on a fresh page. This is your "nugget of truth" for the day. If you're working on a book, use the longer amount of time to write, directly after the previous steps, or, like me, take some time and come back to this step later in the day.

∞ **S–Surrender (1 minute):** Close your journal, shut your laptop or tablet, put your pen down. Trust that the work is complete for now. Release the need for perfection and breathe. Just as we do in Savasana, where the body begins to integrate what it's learned, so too does our story as we leave it for the day.

Option 4: The Mad Scientist (60-180 minutes)

This can take the same amount of time as option 3, but this option is for someone who wants to dip into practice throughout the day. This is what works for me:

∞ **S–Somatics (5-10 minutes):** In the morning or evening, depending on your preference, begin by closing your eyes and bringing awareness to your body. Notice any tension, tingling, or warmth without judgment. *Before pressing play on your chosen online yoga class, take a moment to sense into your body. What does it feel like right now? Where are you holding tension? What* *sensations are present?* This will help you select the type of yoga class you need that day, and how you will approach it.

- ∞ **E–Embody (30-90 minutes):** Directly after the Somatics step, engage in your online yoga class. As you move, consciously feel each pose. Rather than just going through the motions, focus on the stretch, the breath, and the sensations in your body. In Savasana, simply be open to receiving insights, without trying to generate them.

- ∞ **E–Explore (2-10 minutes now, 10-60 minutes later):** After your practice, sit down with your journal and jot down any stand-out ideas or thoughts. Later, when you're ready, work on your memoir, book project, plans, or journal for a longer period of time.

- ∞ **D–Deepen (10-15 minutes):** Review what you've written. Can you identify a single insight, an image, or a powerful idea that emerged? Highlight it, circle it, or rewrite it on a fresh page. This is your "nugget of truth" for the day.

- ∞ **S–Surrender (1 minute):** Close your journal, shut your laptop or tablet, put your pen down. Trust that the work is complete for now. Release the need for perfection and breathe. Just as we do in Savasana, where the body begins to integrate what it's learned, so too does our story as we leave it for the day.

GUIDING ADVICE FOR YOUR S.E.E.D.S. JOURNEY

1. **Strive for consistency over perfection.** It's far more beneficial to engage in a short, consistent practice than to

wait for the "perfect" conditions for a long one. Five minutes of mindful sensing and writing is better than zero minutes.

2. **Listen to your body.** This is paramount. The S.E.E.D.S. system is about honoring your internal wisdom. If your body needs rest, rest. If it craves gentle movement, move.

3. **Embrace non-judgment.** In both your movement and your writing, approach yourself with curiosity and compassion. There's no right or wrong way to feel or to write.

4. **Be patient.** Developing a deeper mind–body connection and accessing your inner stories takes time and practice. Celebrate small shifts and acknowledge your effort.

5. **Find your rhythm.** Experiment with the different options and schedules. What feels good? What fits seamlessly into your day? The system is designed to serve *you*.

6. **Keep a dedicated journal:** Having a special notebook for your *Ink & Asana* S.E.E.D.S. practice can create a sacred space for your reflections and discoveries. I have created a ***S.E.E.D.S. Journal*** that you can use for this, should you choose to. Like the *Ink & Asana Journal*, it's an optional tool to support your journey, and not at all required. If having a dedicated book to help you on your way speaks to you, you can find it here: <u>www.inkandasana.com/books</u>

By planting these S.E.E.D.S. of intention, mindful movement, and reflective writing, you'll cultivate a vibrant inner garden where stories can blossom and your truest self can flourish. Get after it. Your body and your words are waiting.

24

HOLDING TIME
In the Middle of Always

The path of *Ink & Asana* is not a destination to be reached, but an ongoing journey of becoming. It's a commitment to a lifelong practice of curiosity, compassion, and creativity. The antidote to frustration with the state of the world is expression, so embrace the tools you have learned, and the gifts you were born with, and go forth and do amazing things. The doing is the victory, and you have already taken a major leap forward.

However you end up integrating your writing and yoga practice into your daily life, it will change you forever. But it's your path to find. I've shared my experience, advice, and tools to get you started, but I guarantee that you will take it from here and make it something even more incredible—because it will be yours.

Make *Ink & Asana* and the S.E.E.D.S. system fit your life, not the other way around.

If you're called to write, you may have felt like you were weird or the odd one out. Authors can be a different group of people. I encourage you to embrace the weirdness and to love your imperfections and your obsession with the written word. It's your art, you're better for having created it—and so is the world.

Your yoga poses may be wobbly, and, like life itself, imperfect. Revel in the process of learning and the inevitable falls onto your face or your butt. The practice of *Ink & Asana* teaches you that growth only happens when you show up consistently, and stay open to receive its gifts. Release the grip of your perfectionist.

Both yoga and writing build resilience and light you up so that you can bend without breaking and bounce back when setbacks occur. On the mat, you learn to breathe through the discomfort, and on the page you learn to see and reframe your past. These skills translate into the rest of life and are invaluable in navigating the wild ride we're all on. You'll start to see every challenge as an opportunity for deeper understanding and the building of strength.

That first whisper, *Write to her.* My yoga gave me that thought. And it was the courage I'd built through tough times, and an instinct to connect to something bigger than myself, that made me listen to it. Listen to your whispers, no matter how soft they may be. The practice of asana sharpens your ability to hear your own intuition and recognize your voice.

Trust.

Those whispers are your compass, your guide to your most awesome and purposeful life.

Your journey of self-discovery is deeply personal, but it also has the potential to inspire and transform others. As you gain clarity and confidence in your own voice, you may feel a calling to share your insights, your stories, or your unique way of being in the world. Whether through teaching, writing, speaking, or simply living as an example, your light can illuminate the path for others. Remember, the legacy you build isn't just for yourself; it's a gift to the collective.

Identify a group of people, however small or large, who not only are interested in the same pursuits of yoga and writing as you are but also understand and have been where you have been. While each of us has unique experiences to share, it's nice to know that others were new at one point, or felt unsure of themselves, couldn't hold a balance, or couldn't think of a thing to write. And beyond common understanding, your community is your inspiration—a team of people interested in your development and success. Find your community online or in your neighborhood, but make a point to connect.

I can't wait to see what happens when you give us your thoughts, your insights, and your actions—when you put your story through the wash, and emerge with clear vision, changed. What will your story do next? Will it help at least one person? I sincerely believe so.

The invitation of *Ink & Asana* is to discover your wonder, find yourself, get weird, let go, and live consciously.

And with that, there's only one more word I have left to give.

Begin.

Holding Time

Time is a flowing river that carries everything away, but a book that you write about your life, loves, and lessons—even if only for yourself—is the anchor you drop to hold it still. When you reach the end of this journey, you are not just closing a cover; you are sealing a vessel. You have caught the light of a soul and held it in the permanence of ink. You are now the Middle of Always—a treasure of words that ensures while seasons may pass, your truth—your uniqueness—remains unshakeable.

The Somatic Inquiry:

Lie down in a final Savasana, or sit comfortably in a chair. Let every muscle melt. Feel the weight of time being supported by the earth. Realize that you do not have to hold it all anymore; the page is holding it for you. The burden of forgetting is lifted. The light of your love is gifted. Take a deep breath in... and exhale. You are complete.

INVITATION

The Practice doesn't end here.

You have the tools. You have the map. Now, let's begin this amazing journey together. You can find links to all of the programs below at **www.inkandasana.com/book-bonus**

Step 1: Join the Community

Join the *Ink & Asana* community on Instagram @inkandasana.studio and Facebook @inkandasana

Access the **practice vault** & join me for yoga, meditation, and writing. https://inkandasana.com/vault
(30-Day Free Trial with code NEWMEMBER)
Tiered memberships: choose from on-demand self-led only, or subscribe to on-demand + live sessions.

Step 2: Heal & Grow

Nervous System Rewire: Learn the essentials of nervous system regulation. This self-paced 4-week course will help you establish your *Ink & Asana* practice and rewire (not just reset) your nervous system.

Step 3: Go Deep

Write Your Story: Choose from a self-paced course that deepens your yoga and helps you write your memoir, or a month-to-month private mentorship where you'll work with me 1:1 to develop your practice and your memoir.

Retreat: Learn about upcoming Ink & Asana retreats. Beautiful and inspiring locations to immerse yourself in the practice of writing and yoga.

ACKNOWLEDGEMENTS

To my husband, Ricky, whose relentless support of me never wavers, never fails to help me see that all things are possible—my most skilled off-the-ledge talker, and partner in every way. When working on a project, my passionate nature puts me into "mad scientist" mode, and I thank you for your understanding and encouragement every single step of the way. If I ever start to lose my belief in myself, I can still believe in *your* belief in me. Me, you, you, me.

To my mother, whose enduring inspiration infuses me with forward motion every day of my life. I've had a wonderful life, and so very much of that is because of you. It was writing about our history that made me realize it's not over, and our bond is never-ending. You are the wind, sea, and sun.

To Gramma, I miss you every day. And can you believe this? Wherever you are, your bare feet are kicked up as you relax in your easy chair, and I hope this makes you proud.

To my dad, brother Jeff, and sister-in-love Claudine, your support of my everlasting weirdness is fuel for my fire. And to my niece Elena and nephew Paul, the stories are all told for you, my loves. Stay weird.

Thank you to Claire Dunn for proofreading.

As noted throughout this book, I take inspiration from my master teachers, Bernie Clark and Eoin Finn. The work that you do transforms lives, including my own, and I can only hope my teaching reflects a little of your wisdom and trail-blazing insights. I thank you for your training programs and all that you do for the yoga community.

ABOUT THE AUTHOR

Laura Cole is a certified yoga teacher, the founder of Ink & Asana™, and a Senior Vice President at a global staffing firm. For over a decade, Laura has navigated the high-pressure world of corporate leadership while privately battling chronic illness and the weight of grief. It was in the midst of a descent into a health crisis that she began writing letters to her late mother—a practice that evolved into a lifeline and, eventually, a methodology. Laura's work is built on the belief that yoga and writing are not just tools for healing, but the very foundation for nervous system regulation. By integrating somatic movement with reflective inquiry, she helps practitioners create the internal space necessary for creativity to thrive. When she isn't SVP'ing or teaching yoga and writing, Laura is a painter and a lover of all things nature. She lives in Florida with her husband, dedicated to the practice of being a student first, and a witness always.